HANDBOOK OF

FORENSIC SCIENCE

FEDERAL BUREAU OF INVESTIGATION

Revised August, 1975   FBI Laboratory

Books for Business
New York-Hong Kong

Hanbook of Forensic Science

by
Federal Bureau of Investigation (F. B. I.)

ISBN: 0-89499-073-X

FORWARD

Each day the modern crime laboratory attempts to discover new techniques of applying recent technological and scientific developments to aid the on-the-scene investigator in solving crime. The Handbook of Forensic Science seeks to familiarize the investigator with these techniques and to make known the capabilities and the limitations of the crime laboratory.

The value of properly collected physical evidence examined by trained scientists in the crime laboratory cannot be overestimated. It is a vital element in our criminal justice system.

At crime scenes every law enforcement officer shares the responsibility of collecting as much pertinent physical evidence as possible. The objective of the Handbook is to make available to law enforcement personnel a guide to legally accepted and practical procedures for collecting, preserving and handling physical evidence. It contains suggestions and is offered as a training aid for those in professional law enforcement.

It is hoped that this Handbook will promote maximum use of physical evidence in our criminal justice system and encourage greater use of the crime laboratory to help solve today's law enforcement challenges.

Clarence M. Kelley
Director, FBI

CONTENTS

PART I

INTRODUCTION

I. Nature and value of physical evidence. For the most part, physical evidence falls into two classifications:

    A. Evidence with <u>class characteristics only</u>.

        1. Such evidence, no matter how thoroughly examined, can only be placed into a class. A definite identification can never be made since there is a possibility of more than one source for the material found.

        2. Examples:
            a. Single-layered paint, such as from a safe or car.
            b. Soil.
            c. Glass fragments too small to match broken edges.
            d. Toolmarks, shoe prints, bullets (in instances where microscopic or accidental markings are insufficient for positive identification).
            e. Hairs and fibers.
            f. Blood.
            g. Minute sawdust-sized pieces of wood allowing for species identification only.

    B. Evidence with <u>individual identifying characteristics</u>.

        1. Such evidence can definitely be identified with a person or source if sufficient microscopic or accidental markings are present.

        2. Examples:
            a. Fingerprints.
            b. Handwriting.
            c. Bullets.
            d. Toolmarks.
            e. Shoe prints.
            f. Pieces of glass where broken edges can be matched
            g. Wood where broken/cut surfaces can be matched.

II. It is, of course, desirable to have evidence that can be positively identified, but <u>the value of evidence with class characteristics only should not be minimized</u>. With evidence of this type, the following are desirable:

A. A preponderance of such evidence.

B. A preponderance of identifying features within such evidence.

    1. Paint with many layers, all matching.

    2. Building materials, including brick, mortar, plaster, paint, insulation, glass and soil.

    3. Soil with foreign matter, such as paint chips, odd seeds (sometimes even safe insulation).

C. Elimination specimens.

    1. Soil from where suspect claims he was or where he claims a car was.

    2. Soil from surrounding areas to show that a variation does exist.

    3. Paint or other materials from source mentioned in alibi.

D. Other evidence where class characteristics are in some way unique, such as in an Alaskan case where white stucco was on pry bar in possession of suspect apprehended fleeing area. Officers testified burglarized building was the only white stucco building in town.

III. Services of FBI Identification Division:

A. Largest collection of identification data in the world available to law enforcement agencies.

B. Will furnish standard forms such as fingerprint cards for submitting identification data.

C. Search of fingerprints.

    1. Arrest cards.

    2. Applicant cards (taken in compliance with local statute).

3. Deceased and amnesia victims.

4. International exchange of fingerprint data.

D. Name checks to locate identification records.

E. Fugitive program.

    1. Wanted notices placed on fingerprint cards for law enforcement agencies.

    2. Records of fugitives furnished to agencies.

F. Missing persons program.

    1. Placed for law enforcement agencies.

    2. Placed for relative of the person under certain circumstances.

G. Latent print examinations.

    1. Will examine original evidence, lifts and photographs

    2. Comparisons on case made for indefinite period.

    3. Examinations and comparisons by highly trained experts.

    4. Expeditious service available.

    5. Technical assistance in special situations, such as kidnapping, hijacking cases and airline disasters.

    6. Latent print testimony.

    7. No restriction on prior examination of latent material by other fingerprint technicians.

H. Examination of fingers of deceased persons for possible identification.

I. Reference files in Latent Fingerprint Section.

    1. General appearance file.

            2. Single fingerprint file.
            3. National Unidentified Latent file.

    J. Advanced Latent Fingerprint Schools

    K. Disaster Squad.

            1. Long experience in major disasters.
            2. Speeds identification.

    L. Supplies of literature on identification matters.

IV. Services of the FBI Laboratory:

    A. Capabilities in wide range of forensic sciences under
        following sections:

            1. Document.
            2. Physics and Chemistry.
            3. Cryptanalysis-Gambling-Translation.
            4. Radio engineering.

    B. Examination by highly trained scientists.

    C. Full range of scientific equipment available.

    D. Expeditious service, if needed.

    E. Competent expert testimony.

    F. Technical assistance in special situations, such as
        kidnapping cases, airline disasters, and photographic
        problems.

    G. Standard reference files and collections. Among them:
        typewriter standards, automotive paint, firearms, hairs
        and fibers, blood sera, safe insulation, shoe print, tire
        tread.

    H. Files of questioned material.

            1. National Fraudulent Check File.
            2. Bank Robbery Note File.

V. FBI Identification Division and Laboratory facilities are available:

A. To all federal agencies, U.S. attorneys, military tribunals, in both civil and criminal matters.

B. To all duly constituted state, county and municipal law enforcement agencies in the U.S. in connection with their official criminal investigative matters only.

C. All Identification Division and Laboratory services, including the loan of their experts, if needed as expert witnesses, are rendered free of all cost to the contributing agency.

D. In offering these services, the following considerations are to be noted:

1. Laboratory Division

As a general rule, examinations are not made by the FBI Laboratory if the evidence is subjected elsewhere to the same examination for the Prosecution. However, if the circumstances in a given instance are such that this restriction poses a significant obstacle to an orderly prosecution, these facts should be set forth in a request for waiver. Such requests will be evaluated on a case-by-case basis.

2. Identification Division

Because of the nature of the evidence submitted for fingerprint examination, the above-mentioned Laboratory restriction does not apply. Therefore, the Identification Division will examine fingerprint evidence even if it has been or will be subjected to examination by other fingerprint experts.

3. Testimony

FBI experts will furnish testimony regarding evidence they have examined. In the interest of economy, however, their testimony should not be requested if it is to be duplicated by another Prosecution expert. It is realized that exceptions to this general policy may be required, in a given instance.

E. Detailed information relating to proper methods of handling specific types of evidence will be dealt with in the appropriate sections of this handbook.

PART II

FBI IDENTIFICATION DIVISION

I. The Identification Division of the FBI is the national
    repository of criminal identification data. The obvious
    need and demand by police officials led to an Act of
    Congress establishing, on July 1, 1924, the Identification
    Division. The fingerprint records of both the National
    Bureau of Criminal Identification and of Leavenworth
    Penitentiary, totaling 810,188 were consolidated to form
    the nucleus of the FBI files.

    A. Concerned with fingerprint records and inquiries
        pertinent thereto.

    B. Largest and most useful collection of identification
        data in the world.

    C. Information available to law enforcement agencies and
        officials.

    D. All records and information relating thereto are
        classified as confidential.

    E. Over 159,000,000 criminal and civil prints representing
        60,000,000 persons are in file.

II. Will furnish standard forms for submitting identification
    data.

    A. Advantages:

        1. Saves time of FBI personnel as forms and information
            received are uniform.

        2. Saves time of contributor in writing letters or
            requests.

        3. Insures inclusion of essential data.

    B. Forms available:

        1. Pre-addressed criminal fingerprint cards (Form FD 249
            redesigned 4-26-71).

        2. Applicant fingerprint cards (Form FD 258).

6

3. Personal identification fingerprint cards (Form FD 353).

4. Pre-addressed postage and fees prepaid.

5. Disposition sheets (Form R 84). To subsequently furnish final disposition to an arrest for which a fingerprint card was previously submitted.

6. Wanted request form (Form I 12). To place or cancel a wanted or flash notice in an individual's record.

7. Death notice form (Form R 88). To submit information relating to death of individual for whom a fingerprint record is known to exist.

8. Requisition form (Form I 178). To order supply of above-mentioned forms.

III. Search of fingerprint cards (should list literal or narrative form of charge rather than by state code citations)

A. In order to achieve uniformity in arrest data stored at the national level and to improve efficiency of the manual identification system, the following policy has been approved by the Attorney General of the United States

1. Fingerprints should not be submitted to the FBI Identification Division in connection with non-serious offenses unless there is a question of identity or a check of Identification Division files is considered necessary for current investigative purposes.

2. Fingerprint cards submitted on non-serious offenses will be searched through Identification Division files and returned to the contributor with results of the search.

3 Non-serious offenses appearing on fingerprint cards returned to contributors will not be posted to identification records.

4. Every identification record furnished will bear an FBI number.

5. Criminal fingerprint cards submitted to the Identification Division for which there will not be a court adjudication (final disposition) will be searched and returned to the contributor along with the results of the search.

6. Non-federal applicant fingerprint cards are searched through the FBI Identification Division files and the records disseminated only after the following requirements have been met:
   a. A state statute must provide for finger-printing as a requisite for the type of applicant position involved or for the type of license to be issued.
   b. All applicant and licensee fingerprints must first be checked through the appropriate state identification bureau or, if no such bureau exists, through a central agency designated for such purpose within the state.
   c. The state bureau or agency handling the finger print card should forward only those prints on which no disqualifying record or substantive information is found locally.

B. Value of records.

1. Provides control of prior offenders or vicious characters.

2. Identifies fugitives from justice.

3. Uncovers criminal information regarding persons seeking employment in law enforcement or Government.

4. Uncovers "habitual criminal law" offenders (three or more prior convictions or felonies).

5. Provides prosecuting attorneys, judges, and parole officers with background of defendants.

6. Identifies dead (homicides, accidental deaths, or deaths from natural causes).
   a. Identification of victim essential to investigation of crime.
   b. Generally essential to prosecution of crime.
   c. Family can be notified.
   d. Military burial rights established.

7. Locates missing persons.
   a. Placed for law enforcement agencies.
   b. Placed for relative of the person under certain circumstances.

8. Identifies victims of amnesia or accidents.

C. Approximately 22,000 fingerprints are received each day. Urgent inquiries and identifications are given expeditious handling.

D. Footprint File.

   1. If arrested person has no fingers, footprints should be taken for record purposes.

   2. Area behind "great" toes are used for classification.

   3. About 400 sets are contained in FBI files.

IV. Name checks to locate identification records (includes aliases and nicknames).

A. Provides investigative leads and background of suspects where fingerprints are not available for search.

B. Locates fingerprint records or possible records of fugitives and missing persons.

C. Adequate data must be furnished on which to make a search.

   1. Name

   2. FBI number, or

   3. Law enforcement agency arrest number, or

4. Armed Forces service number.

5. If item two, three, or four not known then descriptive data including date and place of birth of individual should be furnished.

V. Fugitive program.

A. Wanted notices placed on fingerprint records for law enforcement agencies.

1. Agency notified immediately if individual arrested.

2. Over 138,000 fugitive notices on file with an average addition of 1,500 per month.

3. Approximately 3,500 fugitives identified per month.

B. Records and personal descriptions of fugitives furnished to Agency.

C. One year follow-up procedure to determine if "want is still active.

VI. Missing Persons Program.

A. Placed for law enforcement agencies (no reason required).

B. Placed for relative of person under certain circumstances - must involve genuine interest in person's welfare or welfare of minor children.

C. Fingerprint card located in file, if possible.

D. Name and description placed in name file if no fingerprint available.

E. Complete descriptive data and background data should accompany request.

F. Approximately 5,000 active missing person notices maintained in file.

G. One year follow-up procedure to determine if notice is still active.

VII. Latent Fingerprint Section.

A. Latent print examinations.

1. Will examine lifts, negatives, photographs or original objects for latent prints of value for identification purposes.

2. Will compare latent prints for indefinite period with inked prints of suspects submitted or with named suspects whose prints are contained in our files.
   a. Photographs and negatives of latent prints of value are prepared at time of original examination and retained for future comparisons.
   b. No need to resubmit original evidence when making subsequent requests for comparisons.
   c. All original evidence will be returned to contributing agency unless directed to make some other disposition by the contributing agency.

B. Examination of fingers of deceased persons.

1. Through visual examination or special techniques, FBI fingerprint specialist may derive ten-finger formula which permits file search. The best inked prints obtained from decomposed bodies are often not classifiable.

2. If unable to determine ten-finger formula for file search, will preserve all prints, however fragmentary, for comparison with prints of persons named for this purpose by contributor.

3. All such specimens must be returned to contributor since FBI has no authority to dispose of specimens.

4. When investigating case involving deceased, suggest

following always be done:
a. Take inked fingerprints and palm prints for positive identification and for comparison with latent prints which may subsequently be found.
b. If legible inked prints are not possible, sever hands (with proper authority-usually local coroner) and forward in accordance with shipping instructions in C, **4**, below.

C. Transmitting evidence to FBI Latent Print Section. Refer to page 111 relating to letter of request.

1. Nonporous objects should be placed in individual nonporous protective coverings, such as transparent envelopes. If item is fragile, protect from breakage.

2. Porous items should be placed in a protective covering, such as a paper envelope and any number of such items can be placed in one envelope. Cardboard cartons need not be shipped in assembled position, but may be flattened out and covered with a protective wrapper.

3. If evidence is exclusively for fingerprint examination, it should be directed to:

   Director
   Federal Bureau of Investigation
   Washington, D. C. 20537
   Attention: Identification Division
   Latent Fingerprint Section

   If examinations are involved requiring Laboratory <u>and</u> Latent fingerprint examinations, submit to:

   Director
   Federal Bureau of Investigation
   Washington, D. C. 20535
   Attention: FBI Laboratory

4. Send by railway express, air express, registered mail, registered air mail or by personal delivery. If hands or fingers are being submitted, they should be placed in airtight container filled with alcohol or formaldehyde solution.

D. Latent print examinations and testimony.

1. Examination <u>will</u> be made if the same or similar
    evidence in an individual case has been or will
    be subjected to a technical examination for the
    prosecution by other experts in the same scien-
    tific field.

2. Expeditious service will be accorded specific
    evidence, if requested. Such priority treatment
    should be utilized <u>only</u> when absolutely necessary.

3. Examiner will testify at the trial for all federal
    agencies, U. S. Attorneys and military tribunals
    in both civil and criminal matters and for all
    duly constituted state, county and municipal law
    enforcement agencies in connection with their of-
    ficial investigations of criminal matters. (Note
    the previously-mentioned testimony policy on page
    5, D, 3.)

4. In court proceedings other than a trial (prelim-
    inary hearing, grand jury hearing), it is requested
    that the original official report be used in lieu
    of the actual appearance of our expert, if accept-
    able by the court. However, if the report is not
    accepted, our expert will testify at the hearing.

E. Developing Latent Prints.

1. Nonporous or nonabsorbent surfaces, such as glass,
    polished metal, painted or varnished wood, por-
    celain and ceramic tile, are processed using
    fingerprint powders.
    a. FBI recommends use of gray and black
        powders <u>only</u> since other colors and
        types clump between ridges, do not
        adhere as well, or are more difficult
        to photograph than gray or black.
    b. Choose color of powder to contrast
        with color of surface being examined
        with the exception of reflective mirrors,
        glass or polished chrome. FBI recom-
        mends using gray powder only.

c. Do not powder obviously greasy surfaces, wet surfaces, bloody surfaces or prints in dust. Prints on such surfaces can only be photographed.

2. Porous or absorbent surfaces such as paper, cardboard or unpainted wood are processed chemically using the iodine fuming, ninhydrin, and silver nitrate methods since these processes will develop latent prints for longer periods of time and stains may be removed or partially removed from document material.

F. Preservation of latent prints dictates that permanent replicas or photographs for comparison and prosecutive purposes be made.

1. Photographing. It is recommended that all latent prints be photographed before lifting.

2. Lifting.
a. All powder prints should be lifted after photographing.
b. Transparent tape and rubber tape in black and white are generally used to lift the latent print. When transparent tape is used, a color contrasting to the color of the backing card should be used to secure the lift. Use a color rubber tape which contrasts with the color of powder used.

G. Use of Fingerprint camera.

1. Advantages
a. Fixed focus.
b. Has its own light source.
c. Makes natural size photographs and negatives.

2. FBI recommends Kodak Tri-X 16 exposure ($2\frac{1}{4}$" x $3\frac{1}{4}$") film pack.

3. Exposures.
a. Folmor-Graflex camera.
1. Black powder print on white surface-snapshot.

        2. Gray powder on black surface-one second.
    b. Sirchie camera.
        1. Set diaphragm at F.3.
        2. Black powder print on white surface-
one second.
        3. Gray powder print on black surface-
two second.

4. Procedures for use of fingerprint camera.
    a. Camera opening must be flush with surface.
    b. Shut out all outside light.
    c. Take several shots of each latent print with appreciable variations in exposure times (Example: snapshot, one second and two seconds).
    d. Take overlapping shots of large areas such as palm prints or simultaneous fingerprints.
    e. Prints showing definite elevation of ridges and furrows sometime show better contrast by turning out lights on one side of camera.
    f. Position latent prints in center of opening on front of camera. Include identification tag alongside each print to be photographed. This tag should bear initials, date, and other data necessary to identify with crime scene.

H. Reference Files in Latent Fingerprint Section.

1. General Appearance file of confidence men (swindlers) and major thieves contain approximately 1,255 confidence men and 790 major thieves (primarily fur and jewel thieves).
    a. Agency should obtain complete description of subject from victim and forward for search.
    b. Photos of persons having similar description will be forwarded to agency for display to victim.

2. Single fingerprint files contain known prints of persons who have committed certain types of

major crimes. Categories included are:
a. Bank robbery.
b. Bank burglary.
c. Bank larceny.
d. Kidnapping.
e. Extortion.
f. Interstate transportation of obscene materials
g. Major thieves.
h. Professional fraudulent check passers.

3. National Unidentified Latent File contains unidentified latent prints from crime scenes in FBI investigated major-type crimes.

I. Advanced Latent Fingerprint Schools.

1. Latent print examiners will be sent as instructors Submit request to local FBI.
2. FBI will furnish technical equipment.
3. Sponsored by a local law enforcement agency.
4. Desire 15 to 25 local law enforcement officers in each school.

J. FBI Disaster Squad - will assist in identifying victims in major disasters.

1. By fingerprinting victims.
2. By comparing prints of victims with available known prints at scene.
3. Requires request from local law enforcement agency or transportation company.

VIII. Identification Literature.

A. Reprints of articles previously appearing in Law Enforcement Bulletin on detailed aspects of latent print work and general Identification Division matters

B. Booklet of standard arrest abbreviations.

C. Booklet "Science of Fingerprints" available through the FBI or the Government Printing Office at a cost of $1.00 (economical and best textbook).

PART III

FBI LABORATORY DIVISION

SEROLOGY

I. Introduction:

Analyses of blood and other body fluids are made in the
Serology Unit of Laboratory. Evidence is received mainly
in connection with violent crimes, such as murder, rape,
robbery, assault-and-battery. Evidence in burglary, hit-
and-run and game violation cases also frequently received.

II. Specific ways in which blood examinations may aid in
investigations.

A. In location of crime scene:

Identification of human blood of similar group to
victim can pinpoint area for crime search.

B. In determining possible commission of crime:

Occasionally, the identification of human blood on a
highway, sidewalk, porch, or in a car is the first
indication of a crime's occurrence.

C. In identifying weapon used:

The grouping of human blood identified on a club,
knife or hammer can be of considerable investigative
and prosecutive value.

D. In proving or disproving suspect's alibi:

The findings of human blood on an item belonging to
a suspect who claims an animal as the blood source.
The finding of animal blood can substantiate the claim
of an innocent person.

E. In eliminating suspects:

The determination by grouping tests that human blood
on suspect items is different from the victim's
blood can facilitate the release of a suspect.
Blood found similar to the suspect's blood group can
help to substantiate a suspect's claim of having a
nosebleed or other injury.

III. Information determinable by blood tests:

A. Identification of stains as blood:

Chemical and microscopic analyses are necessary to positively identify blood. The appearance of blood can vary greatly depending on the age of stains and on other factors.

B. Determination whether blood is of human or animal origin.

1. If animal, determination of specific animal family.

2. If human, classification of dried blood into one of four major groups of "O," "A," "B," and "AB," in order of incidence. Additionally, blood may be subgrouped as "M," "N" or "MN" and the RH factors may be determined. These latter sub-groupings are dependent on the age of the stain.

IV. Limitations of blood examinations:

A. It is not possible to identify human blood as coming from a particular person.

B. The race and sex of the person from whom blood came cannot be ascertained; nor can age of dried stain be determined.

V. Collection, identification and wrapping of bloodstained evidence:

A. Garments and fabrics:

1. Investigator's identifying marks should be put directly on fabric in ink, away from stained areas if possible.

2. Each item should be wrapped separately.

3. Stains which are moist must be dried out before wrapping or putrefaction of blood will occur.

Drying should be done by exposure to atmosphere in secure, well-ventilated room and not be exposed to sunlight or heat.

B. Blood on surfaces such as walls or floors:

Can be scraped off into pillbox or vial. If envelope only is available, scrapings should be first enclosed in druggist fold and thoroughly sealed by cellophane tape. Container identified by investigator's marks.

C. Blood on auto surfaces:

1. If not present in sufficient quantity to scrape off, stained car unit should be submitted.

2. Identifying data can be scratched into metal.

D. Blood on pieces of glass:

1. Pieces should be submitted if stains are too thin for removal of adequate amount by scraping.

2. Specimens should be insulated in package to avoid breakage in transit.

3. Mark item itself or on container holding scrapings.

E. Blood in dirt or sand:

1. If blood is encrusted on surface, the crusts should be removed and enclosed in separate pillboxes to avoid contamination with dirt and sand during shipment. Remainder of specimen may be submitted in circular ice cream-type container.

2. Mark containers appropriately.

F. Blood on large metallic objects, such as car bumpers or pipes:

1. If shipped in wooden box, the use of wooden cleats or wires inside box is suggested to hold specimen securely and avoid frictional removal of stains during shipment.

2. Mark items themselves.

G. Liquid blood samples:

1. Samples from victim and suspect should be submitted, if obtainable.

2. Sample should be at least five cubic centimeters in a properly marked sterile container.

3. No refrigerants should be used.

4. A small amount of an anticoagulant is recommended.

5. Sample should be shipped <u>registered airmail special delivery</u> to the Laboratory.

6. Stopper should be sealed with tape to avoid loosening due to air pressure differences in plane and possible loss of blood.

VI. Blood evidence transmittal letter should include following information:

A. Any claims made by suspect as to source of blood on evidence items.

B. Blood group of victim and suspect, if definitely known.

C. Whether or not suspect was injured and mixture of blood exists.

D. Whether or not animal blood might be present.

VII. Other significant body fluids:

A. Seminal stains:

1. Their identification by chemical and microscopic means on vaginal smears or swabs or on rape victim's clothing may be of value in corroborating claims of victim.

2. If secretor, can determine blood group (note C on next page).

B. Saliva stains:

   If present on clean nonfilter-tip cigarette butts
   found at scene, may be of value for blood grouping
   tests, if smoker was secretor (note C below).

C. Differentiation between secretors and nonsecretors:

   1. Secretor - one of about 80% of population who
       has in his other body fluids the same blood
       group factors which are present in his blood.

   2. Nonsecretor - one of minority who does not have
       blood group factors in his other body fluids.

D. Limitations on seminal stain and saliva stain
    grouping tests:

   1. Too often semen is mixed with urine or vaginal
       secretions of victim and reliable grouping tests
       are not possible.

   2. Saliva on cigarette stubs often dirty. Saliva
       on cigar butts is not groupable.

   3. A person may be a "weak" secretor and the amount
       of blood group factor present in the semen or
       saliva is insufficient for reliable grouping tests

MICROSCOPIC ANALYSIS

I. Types of examinations conducted by this Unit:

   A. Hairs

   B. Fibers

   C. Fabric

   D. Tape

   E. Cordage

   F. Laundry marks

   G. Unknown skeletal remains

   H. Miscellaneous types of examinations (see Part VII, E)

II. Value of hair and fiber examinations. While hair and fiber examinations are circumstantial from an evidentiary standpoint, they can corroborate other evidence or testimony and assist in:

   A. Placing perpetrator at scene of crime through:

      1. Interchange of hair and fibers between victim's and assailant's clothing in crimes of violence such as rape, assault and murder.

      2. Hairs and fibers from suspect left at scene of crime such as burglaries, armed robberies and car thefts.

   B. Identifying scene of crime:

      Torn clothing or hairs of suspect or victim left at scene.

   C. Identifying weapon or instrument of crime:

      Hairs and fibers on wrenches, knives, or clubs.

   D. Identifying hit-and-run vehicles:

      Hairs and fibers adhering to suspect automobile.

III. Limitations of hair and fiber examinations:

A. Due to minute size of this type evidence, sometimes very difficult to locate.

B. Not suitable for initial screening of many possible suspects.

IV. Hair examinations:

A. What Laboratory can determine from a single hair:

1. Whether animal or human:
   a. If animal: the species from which it originated such as horse, cat, dog or deer.
   b. If human;
      1. Race of person originated from. Whether Negroid, Caucasian, Mongoloid or mixture of two or more.
      2. Body area hair originated from - head, pubic, chest, limb.
      3. How hair was removed from body. Whether fell out naturally or forcibly removed.
      4. Whether hair is damaged by having been cut, crushed or burned.
      5. Whether hair is altered in any manner, such as being bleached or dyed.
      6. Natural or artificially waved.

2. Cannot tell sex or age from examination of hairs.

B. Hair comparisons:

1. Can compare hairs found on victim's clothing, in victim's hand or on hit-and-run automobile, with known sample of hair from suspect or victim.

2. Adequate sample of hair from suspect or victim for comparison purposes should consist of at least 12 full-length hairs from different areas of head and the same from pubic region, if appropriate to case. These hairs should be pulled or clipped as close to the skin as possible. In rape cases, pubic hair combings should be obtained prior to taking above samples.

3. Results of hair comparisons:
    a. Hairs match in microscopic characteristics and originated either from same individual or from another individual of same race whose hairs exhibit the same microscopic characteristics.
    b. Hairs are dissimilar and did not originate from same individual.
    c. No conclusion could be reached.

V. Fiber examinations:

A. Identification of type of textile fiber:

    1. Animal, as in woolen fibers.

    2. Vegetable, as in cotton fibers.

    3. Synthetic, as in nylon fibers.

    4. Mineral, as in glass fibers.

B. Determination as to whether or not questioned fibers are same type, color and match in microscopic characteristics those fibers composing a suspect garment. Note that color and microscopic characteristics of fibers may vary on garment due to many factors, such as wear or fading.

C. A fiber match is not positive evidence, but circumstantial and must be supported by other evidence.

D. Fiber identifications utilize:

    1. Microscopic examination.

    2. Microchemical examination.

    3. Instrumental examination.

E. Submit entire garment for examination.

VI. Fabric examinations:

Fabric is composed of woven or knitted yarns. These yarns are composed of fibers twisted together. A Laboratory can:

A. Determine the composition and construction of the yarn.

B. Determine whether or not the questioned fabric is like the known fabric.

C. Sometimes a positive identification can be made if a questioned piece of fabric can be fitted to known fabric. For instance, if a button adhering to a small piece of fabric can be fitted back to the garment from which it was torn.

VII. Other types of examinations conducted by the Microscopic Analysis Unit:

A. Tape examinations:

1. Similar to fabric examination.

2. Piece of tape left at scene of crime can be matched to suspect roll, providing another piece of tape has not subsequently been torn from roll.

3. Do not wad tape into ball when recovered since this frequently distorts the ends.

4. Be alert to presence of fingerprints on tape.

B. Cordage examinations:

1. Determine composition, construction, color, diameter.

2. Comparison of known rope with questioned rope.

3. If ends of rope not too frayed, can sometimes match end of questioned rope to known rope.

4. Manufacturer can <u>sometimes</u> be determined, if tracer present.

C. Laundry mark examinations:

    1. Invisible Laundry Mark File maintained in Labora-
        tory. Source usually can be determined.

    2. Military laundry marking formerly consisted of
        first letter of serviceman's last name followed
        by last four digits of his service number.
        Social Security Number now used.

D. Skeletal remains:

    1. Animal or human.

    2. If human; race, sex, approximate height and
        stature, approximate age at death and approximate
        time lapse since death may be determined.

    3. Frequent identifications made through markings
        in clothing fragments, comparison of teeth with
        dental records and old bone fractures with X rays.

E. Miscellaneous examinations:

    1. If fabrics cut or torn

    2. Broken button matches

    3. Glove prints

    4. Fabric impressions

    5. Wood specimens

    6. Plant material

    7. Cigarette butts

    8. Night depository trap devices

599-243 O - 75 - 3

VIII. Collection, preservation and transmittal of hair and fiber evidence:

A. Items, such as clothing, to be examined for hairs and fibers.

1. Avoid contamination:
   a. Do not place victim's and suspect's clothing on same table.
   b. Wrap each item separately; upon removal, if possible.

2. Identify each garment by placing your initials directly on garment.

B. Microscopic evidence such as hairs and fibers recovered at scene should be:

1. Placed in a pillbox or in a piece of paper folded into a druggist's fold.

2. Never place this type of evidence in an envelope without being wrapped first.

3. Do not secure hairs or fibers to paper by means of transparent tape.

4. Initial container for identification purposes.

MINERALOGY

I. Introduction:

"Mineralogy," as used here, covers a wide range of materials and substances which are all or in part mineral in nature.

II. Value of mineral evidence is in assisting to:

A. Place a suspect or object at the crime scene.

B. Prove or disprove a suspect's alibi.

C. Provide investigative leads.

III. Types of examinations:

A. Soils:

1. Soils change in mineral and organic content usually within a short distance. A change in the color of the soil is significant.

2. Soil on shoes, clothing, tools, and other objects may help in placing a suspect at a crime scene in rape, assault, murder, burglary and related cases.
   a. Collect several soil specimens at the scene from likely spots. Place about one cup full from the ground surface in a leakproof container. Do this for each specimen.
   b. Collect specimens from 100' to 100 yards on four sides of the crime scene to aid in delineating soil areas.

3. An automobile acquires characteristic soils on the fenders and frame usually different from soils on other automobiles. In hit-and-run cases, the soil left at the scene may be assoicated with a particular automobile.
   a. Obtain separate soil specimens from the frame and each fender of a suspect vehicle.
   b. Dirty grease under vehicle is treated as a soil in the Laboratory.

B. Safe insulations:

Insulating materials placed between the steel walls of
safes or composing the walls of vaults.

1. Particles in the clothing of suspect.

2. Deposits on tools and objects.

3. Debris in vehicles.

4. Obtain several lumps of insulation from the burglar-
    ized safe. Place in a leakproof container.

C. Building materials:

Concrete, mortar, brick, plaster, insulations and others

1. Usually found in connection with entry
    through wall or roof.

2. Particles in clothing of suspects.

3. Deposits on tools.

4. Debris in automobiles.

5. Obtain representative specimens of each of the
    materials composing the wall, roof or ceiling
    at the point of entry. Place in a leakproof con-
    tainer, identify and seal.

D. Dust and debris:

1. Dust from windowsills and skylights on clothing.

2. Dust and debris on stolen objects compared with
    dust and debris at the crime scene.

3. Dust and debris on clothing indicative of a
    specific occupation may provide investigative leads.

4. Characteristic dusts; asbestos, coal, flour, abra-
    sives.

5. Obtain dust specimens from windowsills or other
    areas by brushing a quantity into a leakproof con-
    tainer, identify and seal.

E. Glass particles:

Glasses from different sources usually vary in physical and optical properties.

1. Glass particles from broken windows, door and auto-mobile windows may be found on clothing, tools, and objects in possession of suspects.
2. If more than one pane of glass is broken, specimens of each should be obtained.
3. Hit-and-run cases:

Glass at the scene and on clothing of victim may be associated with a suspect vehicle.

F. Rocks, ceramics, ores, minerals and precious stones.

G. Abrasives:

1. May be involved in malicious damage, sabotage and safe burglary cases.
2. Grinding wheels, loose grit and liquids.

H. Botanical examinations are made of plant materials, often is connection with soil examinations. Known plants from suspected areas should be submitted for comparisons.

IV. Collection of evidence:

A. Dry clothing and shoes before wrapping to prevent mildew.

B. Identify and wrap each article of clothing and each object in a separate wrapper. Avoid any possibility of leakage or contamination.

C. Place dirty grease and oil in leakproof glass or plastic container. Seal and identify.

D. Loose materials such as soil, safe insulation, building materials, dust, glass and abrasives should be individually placed in strong, leakproof containers, sealed and identified.

E. Never use envelopes for loose materials.

F. Pack to prevent breakage in transit.

CHEMICAL EXAMINATIONS

The Analytical Chemistry Unit deals with the composition of different kinds of materials submitted for examination to the Laboratory. This Unit covers those operations performed to determine the constituents of a chemical compound. Analytical chemical examinations may be <u>qualitative</u> and are made for determining the nature of the constituents, or what is present. <u>Quantitative</u> chemical analysis deals with the methods for determining in what proportion, or how much of the constituents are present.

The three major areas of work in Analytical Chemistry performed in this Unit are:

      I.   Toxicology
     II. Pharmacology
   III. General Chemistry

I. Toxicology:

   A. Definition:

      Scientific study of poisons, their actions, detection and treatment of conditions produced by them.

   B. Source of materials for examination:

      1. Medicolegal Autopsy:

         At post mortem examination of deceased, the liver, brain, kidneys, stomach, stomach contents, blood and urine are removed.

      2. Animal poisonings.

      3. Food and drink.

   C. Preserving and packing specimens:

      1. Refrigeration. Use dry ice packed around containers holding specimens.

      2. Avoiding contamination of specimens. Pack in separate glass or plastic containers.

      3. Chemical preservatives should not be used.

D. Collateral sources of information:

    1. Autopsy report. A running account of surgeon's observations in his examination of the body.

    2. Other leads from investigation, such as eyewitness reports, medical history, hospital treatment.

E. Methods of examination:

    1. Volatile poisons. Distillation removes alcohols, ethers, chloroform and similar substances.

    2. Extraction of poisons by organic solvents. Alcohol-soluble poisons. Tissues are extracted with solvents to remove barbiturates, alkaloids, analgesics and other drugs.

    3. Metals. Tissue specimens are examined chemically and instrumentally to identify metal traces.

    4. Others. Special methods are used for poisons not in three main groups. Carbon monoxide is typical example of this class.

II. Pharmacology:

A. Definition: Science which deals with study of drugs in all their aspects.

B. Sources of materials. In general, pharmaceuticals include most substances in this **class** of materials. Narcotics and a few crude drugs are also included, such as marijuana.

C. Sources of information concerning specimens:

    1. Interview of suspect regarding source, use and effects.

    2. Prescription numbers and other information on containers.

D. Methods of examination. The methods used are generally the same as those used for identification of poisons (Part I. E, 2).

E. Methods of collection and preservation:

   1. Each item should be packaged separately and securely and the package sealed.

   2. Each item, or its containers, should be clearly identified by initials and item number.

III. General chemical examinations:

   A. Definition: Examination of miscellaneous materials of a chemical nature.

   B. Sources of materials. Items of evidence from cases involving fraud, malicious mischief, sabotage, assaults or arson.

   C. Sources of information concerning specimens to be examined. Specifications, circumstances and any information developed by investigation.

   D. Methods of collection and preservation:

   1. Each item should be packaged separately and securely and the package sealed.

   2. Each item, or its containers, should be clearly identified by initials and item number.

GLASS FRACTURES

I. Introduction:

Fragments of glass found at the scene of a burglary, murder, or hit-and-run accident can often be the determining factor in the solution of such cases.

II. Determining directions of a bullet through a pane of glass:

When a bullet passes through glass, a cone-shaped hole is formed as shown below. The big portion of the cone is on the exit side. If this cone is present, the direction of flight is easily established. Unfortunately, the impact force of the bullet often blows this coned area out. When this occurs, determination is made by stress line configuration described on next page.

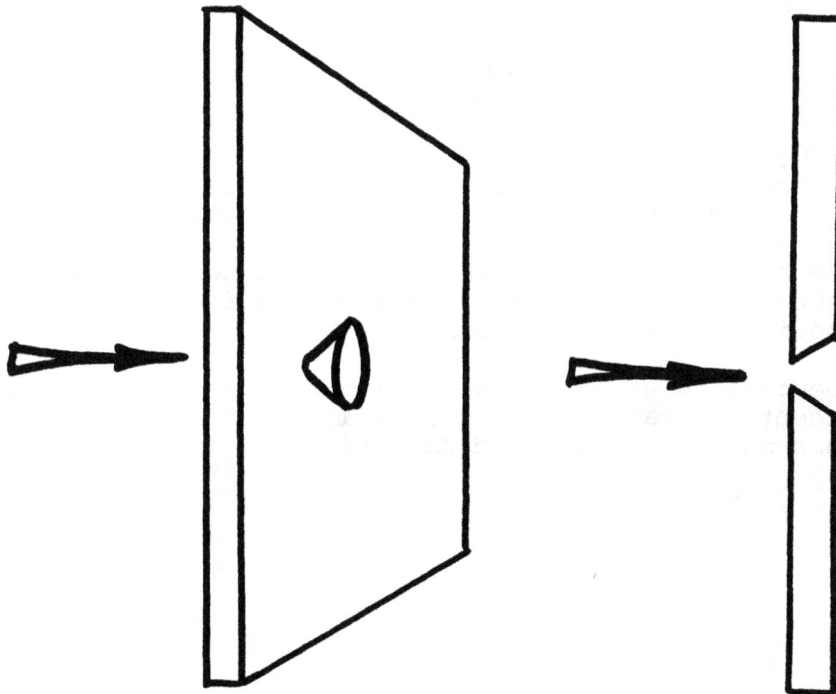

III. Determining direction of blow against pane of glass:

A. When glass breaks, a series of radial and concentric cracks are found about the point of impact.

B. Radial cracks radiate out from the point of impact while concentric cracks form a rough circle or circles around the point of impact. The resulting piece of glass is generally pie shaped.

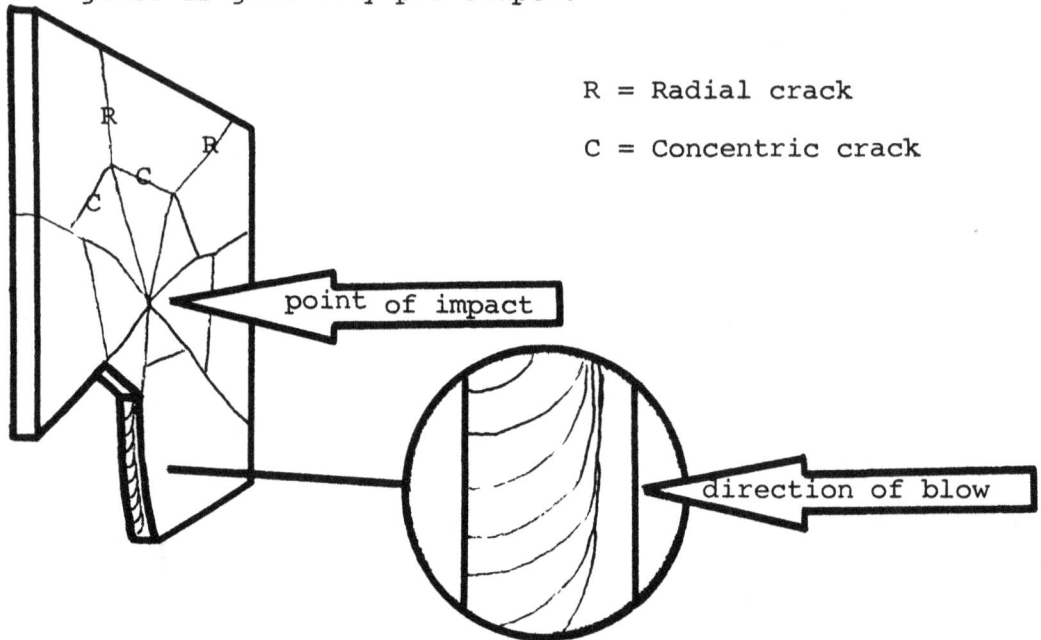

R = Radial crack

C = Concentric crack

point of impact

direction of blow

C. On the fractured edges of the glass pieces, a series of stress lines are formed which tend to be parallel to one face and perpendicular to the other.

D. On a radial crack edge these stress lines will be at right angles to the rear surface (the face of the glass opposite to the one struck).

E. Essential to establish which are radial and which are concentric cracks. Therefore, all available pieces of glass must be used for examination.

36

IV. Positive identification of glass fragments.

When glass fragments are large enough they may be positively identified as having originated from a specific source, such as a broken windowpane or bottle.

V. Fragments of glass found at scene of hit-and-run accident:

A. Type and manufacturer of headlights.

B. Year and make of car, if parking lights or taillight lens. In recent years these are no longer composed of glass in most vehicles, but such examinations can still be conducted.

C. Positive identification of pieces from scene with suspect car.

VI. Submitting glass specimens to the Laboratory:

A. Submit all available.

B. Carefully pack to prevent breakage.

C. If direction of blow examination is desired, label window frame or glass remaining in window as to inside and outside before removing for shipment to Laboratory.

FIREARMS IDENTIFICATION

I. Introduction:

A. Definitions:

    1. Firearms Identification is primarily the study of microscopic marks appearing on the surfaces of fired bullets, cartridge cases and shotshell casings. It has as its purpose to identify these ammunition components as having been fired by a specific weapon to the exclusion of all other weapons.

    Other related examinations would include gunshot residue tests, shot pattern tests and functional tests of weapons.

    2. Ballistics: The study of the motion of a projectile. It is subdivided into:
        a. Interior Ballistics: The study of the motion of a projectile while still within the confines of the firearm.
        b. Exterior Ballistics: The study of the motion of a projectile after it leaves the firearm and during its flight.
        c. Terminal Ballistics: The study of the effect of the projectile on the target.

B. Basis of science: The microscopic marks are individual and characteristic of a specific weapon and result from:

    1. The tools used in the manufacturing processes which produce the weapon.

    2. The subsequent use and abuse of that particular weapon by its various owners.

These marks are transferred to the softer metal of the ammunition during loading, firing, extracting and ejecting cycles. Microscopic study and comparison will then permit the following conclusions.

C. Conclusions:

    1. The bullet, cartridge case, or shotshell casing was fired by the weapon.

2. The bullet, cartridge case, or shotshell casing was not fired by the weapon.

3. There are not sufficient microscopic marks remaining on the bullet, cartridge case, or shotshell casing to determine if it was fired by the weapon.

When an identification is effected, it is positive as in fingerprint identification.

II. Ammunition: Cartridges and shotshells

    A. Cartridges: Two major categories:

        1. Rimfire - primer material is contained in rim around head of cartridge. Large numbers produced but primarily available in .22 caliber.

        2. Centerfire - primer material located in self-contained primer cup positioned in center of head end of cartridge, as in .38 Special caliber.

    B. Cartridge components:

        1. Bullet

        2. Cartridge case

        3. Powder charge

        4. Primer mixture

        5. Primer cup (excluding rimfire cartridges)

    C. Bullet: The projectile

        1. Composition: Lead, coated lead, jacketed, zinc alloy, magnesium. Pellets are found in shotshells. Such pellets are not identifiable with specific weapon.

2. Design: The design or shape of the bullet is determined by numerous factors such as powder charge, use for which the bullet is intended, best ballistics, type of weapon in which it is to be fired.

3. Cannelures: Grooves around lead bullets and some jacketed bullets used for:
   a. Identification of manufacturer
   b. Identification of bullet weight
   c. Lubrication
   d. Crimping

D. Cartridge Case: The container holding components together subdivided into following types:

1. Rimmed: Full rim as in revolver cartridges.

2. Rimless: No rim as in the caliber .45 Auto cartridge.

3. Semi-rimmed: Very slight rim as in the caliber .25 Auto cartridge.

4. Belted: Built up or reinforced near base or head.

Case component may be straight, tapered, necked, taper necked.

E. Powder Charge: The propellant can be:

1. Smokeless:
   a. Single base: Nitrocellulose gelatinized by a solvent.
   b. Double base: A colloid of nitrocellulose and nitroglycerin.

2. Black powder (little used today):
   a. Charcoal 15%
   b. Sulfur 10%
   c. Potassium nitrate 75%

F. Caliber: In general, caliber denotes the nominal bore diameter of a barrel measured in either hundredths of an inch (.01) or in millimeters (mm). This provides an initial grouping capability, such as referring to .22 caliber, .30 caliber, or .38 caliber.

However, within each group or caliber family there may be numerous cartridges, in many instances not interchangeable.

Of more importance is to establish the <u>specific cartridge designation</u>. These designations expand from the basic caliber grouping in a variety of ways. Among them are the following:

1. Descriptive words: .38 Special, .41 Magnum, .380 Auto, 9mm Corto.
2. Original powder charge: .30-40 Krag.
3. Manufacturer's or designer's name:
    a. .30 Remington, 6mm Remington
    b. .257 Roberts
4. Velocity: .250-3000
5. Year of adoption: .30-06 Springfield
6. Millimeters and length of case: 8 x 57, 7 x 57.

Both rimfire and centerfire normally have manufacturer's markings stamped into the head end of cartridge. These markings are known as the "headstamp." Centerfire headstamp consists of manufacturer's name, initials or trade name and specific caliber type. Caliber .22 rim fire has symbol or trademark.

G. The gun:

1. Revolvers

2. Pistols (frequently called "automatics" but technically auto-loading).

3. Rifles:
    a. Automatic (technically auto-loading)
    b. Pump action
    c. Bolt action
    d. Lever action

4. Machine guns (weapons capable of full automatic fire)

H. Rifling:

1. Series of grooves in the interior surface of the barrel which spiral down its length causing bullet to spin and travel nose forward for accuracy.

2. General rifling characteristics (GRC). Vary from manufacturer to manufacturer and consist of:
   a. Number of lands and grooves.
   b. Their dimensions.
   c. Direction of twist of rifling.

I. Manufacturing processes in barrel manufacture:

   1. Drill

   2. Ream

   3. Rifle:
      a. Hook
      b. Scrape
      c. Broach
      d. Button
      e. Press or cold form (SWAGE)

J. Ejection and extraction: Each weapon has some provision for removing cartridges and cartridge cases which may or may not mark the cartridge or cartridge case.

K. Shotshells: The complete round consisting of following components:

   1. Shot pellets, buckshot or slug load.

   2. Shotshell casing - cardboard or plastic tube with metal at head end.

   3. Primer mixture

   4. Primer cup

   5. Battery cup

   6. Powder charge

   7. Wads - cardboard, plastic, felt, composition, single-unit polyethylene.

L. Markings:

    1. Particular shotshell loading,
        such as: $3-1\frac{1}{4}-7\frac{1}{2}$ where
                       3 - Dram equivalents of powder
                       $1\frac{1}{4}$ - Ounces of shot
                       $7\frac{1}{2}$ - Size of shot

    2. Gauge

    3. Manufacturer's name or trademark

    4. Type of shell

M. Gauge designation: Gauge originally meant the number of equal-sized balls obtainable from one pound of lead, any one of which would fit the bore of the shotgun, Thus, a one-ounce lead ball would fit the bore of a 16 gauge shotgun (exception, .410 gauge).

N. Powder charge: (SEE E)

O. Shotguns:

    1. Single barrel

    2. Double barrel

    3. Automatic (technically auto-loading)

    4. Pump action

    5. Bolt action

    6. Lever action

    7. Combination rifle and shotgun

P. Choke: Constriction at muzzle end of shotgun barrel to control spread of shot pellets.

III. Examinations by Laboratory:

    A. Bullets: Marks on bullets produced by rifling in barrel of weapon or possibly in loading:

        1. Recovered evidence bullet: Determine manufacturer, specific caliber, type and make of weapon from which fired and whether sufficient marks are present for identification. (Make of weapon involved based on general rifling characteristics.)

        2. Bullet versus weapon: Determine whether bullet fired from weapon.

        3. Shot pellets, buckshot and slug load from victim or scene: Can identify size of shot and gauge of slug load. Shot not identifiable with a suspect shotgun.

    B. Fired cartridge case or shotshell casing: Marks on fired cartridge case or shotshell casing can be produced by breech face, firing pin, chamber, extractor and ejector.

        1. Fired cartridge case found at scene: Determine specific caliber, type and possibly make of weapon in which fired, and whether sufficient marks are present for identification.

        2. Fired shotshell casing found at scene: Determine gauge original factory loading and whether sufficient marks are present for identification.

        3. Wadding or shot from victim or scene: From wadding determine gauge and possibly manufacturer of wadding. From shot-determine size. Shot not identifiable with a suspect weapon.

        4. Fired cartridge case/shotshell casing versus weapon: to determine whether loaded into and/or fired in weapon.
            a. Based on identifiable firing pin impression, breech face or chamber marks, can establish as fired in _specific_ weapon.
            b. Based on extractor or ejector marks, can only identify as having been loaded into and extracted from specific weapon.

44

C. Unfired cartridges or shotshells: (See note below regarding "Shipping of Live Ammunition.") Sometimes important to determine whether loaded into and extracted from a weapon based on presence of extractor and/or ejector marks (see B, 4, b). If found at scene, can determine from:

1. Cartridge: Specific caliber, type of weapon involved and whether sufficient marks for identification.

2. Shotshell: Gauge and whether sufficient marks are present for identification.

3. Cartridge/shotshell versus weapon: Determine if loaded into and extracted from a suspect weapon. Does not apply to revolvers.

D. The Laboratory uses a comparison microscope to make a direct side-by-side comparison of fired evidence bullets, cartridge cases, shotshell casings, as well as unfired cartridges and shotshells with tests obtained from a suspect weapon.

E. Other examination:

1. Gunshot residues: (Muzzle - to - garment distance)
    a. Microscopic examination of the area surrounding the hole for gunpowder particles and gunpowder residues, smudging and singeing.
    b. Chemical processing of area surrounding hole to develop a graphic representation of powder residues and lead residues around hole. Test patterns obtained compared with those produced at various distances using suspect weapon and ammunition like that used in the case -- from same source if possible. (See note below regarding "Shipping of Live Ammunition.")

SHIPPING OF LIVE AMMUNITION

Live ammunition cannot be sent through the U.S. Mails, but can be shipped via rail or air by carriers such as Railway Express Agency (REA), Emory, Federal Express, etc

Because live ammunition is classified as a Class C Explosive by the Department of Transportation, special packing and labeling regulations have been issued for both air and rail shipments of live ammunition. (See "Regulations for Shipment of Small Arms Ammunition" excerpted from "Hazardous Materials Regulations of the Department of Transportation -- Tariff 29," p. 132)

Naturally, air shipments are considerably more expedient than rail but both means are costly. Therefore, prior to shipment, a careful evaluation should be made regarding the need to examine recovered cartridges or shot shells, whether found in a weapon, clip or magazine, or other sources. Laboratory examinations of live ammunition are normally limited to cases involving:

    a. extractor or ejector mark comparisons (See C.3. above).
    b. gunshot residue tests (muzzle-to-garment distance determinations) (See E. p. 45).
    c. shot pattern tests (See 3. p. 46).
    d. cases in which reloaded ammunition was used.

2. Paraffin casts:
    a. Former test for nitrates:
        1. A paraffin cast is made of suspect's hands.
        2. Casts are chemically processed to determine if nitrate deposits are present. Such deposits could result from discharging a weapon.

      NOTE: This test is not specific for gunpowder residues and, therefore, not considered valid for determining whether or not an individual has fired a weapon.

    b. Test for barium and antimony: More specific procedure, see section on Neutron Activation Analysis, XI, D, page 67.

3. Shot pattern determinations: Determine distance at which a shotgun was fired. It is necessary to test fire the suspect weapon at various distances using the same type of ammunition as involved in the case being investigated. Fired shotshells from suspect can be submitted. Caution: See note regarding "Shipping of Live Ammunition," and specific packing and labeling regulations, p. 132.

4. Trigger pull: Determine amount of pressure necessary to fire a weapon.

5. Examine to determine if weapon can be fired accidentally.

6. Gun parts found at scene:
   a. Identify type of weapon from which part originated.
   b. Identify a part with an individual weapon.

7. Trace metal detection (8-Hydroxyquinoline test); Test to determine if person has been in contact with metal. No examination by FBI Laboratory. Test is conducted and evaluated in field.

   Evaluation is critical. Must be based on extensive research data and experience.

Submission of evidence:

A. Bullet and/or gun: Registered mail.

B. Live ammunition: Air Express or Railway Express at contributor's expense to and from Washington, D.C. Caution: (See note regarding "Shipping of Live Ammunition" and specific packing and labeling regulations, p. 132.)

C. Firing and submission of test specimens for comparison purposes (Whenever possible, submit the gun to the Laboratory):

   1. Fire into cotton waste

   2. Fire into water

D. Clothing for gunshot residue examination:

   1. Protect each article of clothing at time of removal, and wrap each separately.

   2. Make certain all garments are air-dried in shade before submitting to the Laboratory.

   3. Advise location of shots in victim's body.

Standard reference files in Laboratory:

A. Firearms reference collection

   1. Over 2000 handguns

   2. Over 800 shoulder weapons

B. Standard Ammunition File

C. Reference Fired Specimen File

NOTE: An "Unidentified Ammunition File," "Open Case File" or "Unsolved Crime File" consisting of bullets and cartridge cases recovered from crime scenes, in local matters, is no longer maintained by the FBI Laboratory.

VI. Marking specimens for identification:

A. Bullets: Nose or base. Be alert to foreign materials or impressions on nose, if these could be important to your case.

B. Cartridge cases and shotshell casing: Inside the mouth or side of case near mouth.

C. Firearms:

1. Use common sense based on circimstances.

2. Mark gun inconspicuously, such as within trigger guard.

3. Marking can be script initials or other personal identifying mark -- not an "X."

4. Also string tag gun. Tag should be on caliber, make, model and serial number and investigative notes should reflect how and where gun is marked.

5. Avoid defacing weapon by indiscriminate markings. Mark it as if it were your own.

D. Caution: Evidence must be received in condition in which found.

VII. Disposition of weapons: Primarily relating to FBI cases.

A. Any weapon to be disposed of should be done so by the Laboratory.

B. Laboratory can only dispose of weapons with a waiver of ownership or court order. If such cannot be obtained, see United States Marshal's Manual, Section 709.01 (Prisoner's Property), or Section 322.01 (Abandoned Property). When obtaining a court order, the requesting attorney should be advised to seek an order directing the weapons into the custody of the FBI "for its use or for any other disposition in its discretions".

TOOLMARK IDENTIFICATION

I. Introduction:

    A. Toolmark examinations include, but are not limited to, microscopic studies to determine if a given toolmark was produced by a specific tool. In a broader sense, they also include the identification of objects which:

        1. Forcibly contacted each other.

        2. Have been joined together under pressure for a period of time and then removed from contact.

        3. Were originally a single item before being broken or cut apart.

    The inclusion of these latter areas results from the general consideration that when two objects come in contact, the harder (the "tool") will mark the softer. In this context, the field of firearms identification could be considered as a subdivision within the toolmark identification area. (Saws, files and grinding wheels are generally not identifiable with marks they produce.)

    B. Basis for identification:

        1. Class characteristics: physically identical in shape, size, weight, color.

        2. Individual characteristics:
          a. Manufacturing marks.
          b. Marks derived from use or neglect.

    C. Conclusions:

        1. That the tool produced the toolmark.

        2. That the tool did not produce the toolmark.

        3. That there are not sufficient individual characteristics remaining within the toolmark to determine if the tool did or did not produce it.

        (These same conclusions would also apply to the broader considerations mentioned in Part A, 1, 2 and 3.)

II. Types of examinations:

    A. The toolmark itself (no tools as yet submitted).

        1. Impressions
           a. Type of mark produced by a perpendicular force acting against object. Tool does not move laterally across the object.
           b. Examples - punch, some hammer blows, gripping tools, number alteration stampings.

        2. Scrape marks
           a. Tool moves laterally (scrapes) across object.
           b. Examples - flat-bladed tools such as crowbars, pry bars, screwdrivers, slippage from jawed tools

        3. Shearing or pinching marks
           a. Object is caught between opposing forces of two cutting actions.
           b. Examples: <u>Shearing</u>, where blades pass one another as with scissors or tin snips. <u>Pinching</u>, where blades butt against each other as with wire cutters.

    B. Examination of the toolmark can determine:

        1. Type of tool used (class characteristics).

        2. Size of tool used (class characteristics).

        3. Unusual features of tool (class or individual characteristics).

        4. Action employed by tool in its operation.

        5. <u>Most importantly</u>, if toolmark of value for identification purposes.

    C. The comparison of tool with toolmark:

        1. The examination of tool for foreign deposits such as paint or metal for comparison against marked object.

        2. Establishing of consistent <u>class characteristics</u>.

50

3. Making of several test marks or cuts with tool and microscopic comparison of tests versus marked object. If sufficient microscopic marks present, can identify on <u>individual</u> <u>characteristics</u>.

D. Other related examinations:

1. Fracture type to associate broken bolts, automobile ornaments, tips of knife and screwdriver blades with objects from which broken. Can include metallurgical examination (See Metallurgy, Part IV, A, 6, page 60).
2. Wood related, to associated marks left in wood specimens with tool used to cut them, such as pruning shears and auger bit turnings (See Wood, Part II, A, 3, page 54).
3. Miscellaneous pressure or contact examinations to associate any two objects that were in contact momentarily or for more extended time.
4. Conclusions in these related areas are the same as conventional toolmark examinations (See Part I, C).

II. Safe jobs:

A. Punch

1. Knock combination dial knob off safe.
2. Punch spindle through rear of lockbox.
3. If combination lock not equipped with relocking or other preventive device, this method usually easiest and quickest means of entry.
4. If attempted, spindle contains good marks. If successful, spindle often within safe contents and overlooked by investigator.

B. Peel or pop

1. Terms pretty much synonomous.
2. Generally refers to the peel of the door front plate to expose the locking bars. Bars then forced out of engagement.

C. Rip or Chop

1. Attacks on sides or bottom.
2. Generally employs chisel or axe.
3. Bottoms of many safes use thin metal. Depends on safe weight to protect.

D. Drill

    1. Locking bars or bolt are drilled through.
    2. Requires good knowledge of safe construction and
        location of locking bars.
    3. Drill into lockbox to view gate position on tumblers.

E. Explosives

    1. Nitroglycerine extracted from dynamite, blasting gelatin
        or gelatin dynamite.
    2. Primary hazards of personal danger, obtaining explosive
        material and noise.

F. Torch

    1. Requires use of oxy-acetylene tanks and cutting torch,
        bulky equipment.
    2. Any point on safe can be attacked.
    3. Requires good knowledge of safe if attack against
        locking bars or bolt.
    4. Serial numbers on tanks, torches and gauges often
        traceable.

G. Burning bar

    1. Commercially available but easily fabricated.
    2. Temperatures in excess of oxy-acetylene torch.
    3. Any point of safe can be attacked.
    4. "Sparkler" effect may be visible on safe contents.

H. Other methods

    1. Manipulation
    2. Cut-off wheels
    3. Hydraulic jack
    4. Core bore
    5. Photographic surveillance

NOTE: Be alert to major tools left at crime scene such as
       torch equipment, electromagnetic drills or core boring
       tools. Serialized at factory and traceable through
       distributor, they often contain additional company
       control numbers. Tracing to primary theft can provide
       valuable investigative assistance.

IV. Obtaining evidence in toolmark cases

    A. Most desirable, if possible, submit actual toolmarked area for direct comparison.

    B. If impossible to submit, cast of mark - preferably in plastic - next best. In number restoration cases, Laboratory will routinely make such casts for possible future comparison with marking stamps.

    C. Photographs, though helpful in presenting overall location of mark, are of no value for identification purposes.

    D. Don't forget paint, safe insulation, and samples of any material likely to appear as foreign deposits on tools.

    E. <u>Do</u> <u>not</u> place tool against toolmark for size evaluation.

V. Submitting toolmark evidence to Laboratory.

    A. Pack to preserve and prevent contamination.

    B. Properly identify each item to facilitate court presentation. Consider possible need in court of object from which specimen cut.

    C. Submit tool rather than making test cuts or impressions in field.

    D. Mark ends of evidence which are or are not to be examined.

I. Introduction:

The presence of a suspect at the crime scene can often
be established from a comparison of wood from his clothing, vehicle or possession with wood from the crime scene.

II. Types of examination:

A. Specific source identification:

1. Side or end matching. Based on:
    a. Annular ring patterns.
    b. Appearance characteristics such as those
        resulting from defects, disease, knots or
        unusual patterns as in birds eye maple.
    c. Unique cellular structure patterns.

    Permits identification of suitably-sized wood
    specimens (boards, shortened tool handles, tree
    trunks, limbs or fence posts) with the specific
    source from which they were cut.

2. Fracture matching. Based on random nature of
    separation at time of breaking, wood fragments
    can be fitted into parent wood, such as chips or
    pieces from clubs used in assault cases or
    splinters from tool handles left at crime scene
    matched to handle of suspect's tool.

3. Toolmark matching. Based on a sufficiency of
    microscopic marks on cut wood specimens produced
    by tools such as an axe, pruning shears or auger
    bit, it is possible to identify such specimens
    with the specific cutting tool. NOTE: It is
    normally not possible to associate saw marks
    with a specific saw. (See Toolmark Identification
    Part 11, D, 2 , page 51.)

B. Species Identification:

Based on the cellular structure of sawdust-sized wood
particles, it is possible to identify the species
involved, such as oak, maple, pine or spruce, as being

the same species as wood at the scene of a break-in.
Such sawdust-sized particles might come from the shoes
or clothing of a suspect, from his tool bag or found
adhering to prying or cutting tools. While not
identifiable with a specific source as previously
outlined in Part A, such small particles can establish
another link of circumstantial evidence.

III. Submitting wood specimens to the Laboratory:

  A. Be alert not to dislodge wood particles from clothing
     or tools by careless handling.

  B. It is important that each item of clothing be taken
     separately from the suspect and immediately wrapped
     to prevent contamination by contact with other clothing
     or the floor and also to prevent loss of adhering
     particles in transit.

  C. Submit reasonably large samples. For instance, when
     comparing auger bit turnings which may have fallen
     into a burglar's tool bag with a plywood or other
     type door, it would be desirable to have a piece of
     the door which has been cut out, being certain to
     secure samples of each type of wood drilled as well
     as collecting additional drillings from the ground
     or floor at the scene.

  D. Mark each object or its container.

METALLURGY

I. Introduction:

Metallurgy is that branch of science that deals with the study of metals and alloys.

II. Testing Procedures:

A. Toolmark examination can provide positive identification (See Toolmark Identification Section). If not possible in a given case, following are utilized.

B. Physical tests:

1. Measurements

2. Appearance

C. Mechanical tests:

1. Tensile strength

2. Hardness

D. Metallography, a branch of metallurgy, is the science concerning the constitution and structure of metals and alloys as revealed by the microscope. Among influencing factors are:

1. Crystal structure:
   a. Heat treatment
   b. Mechanical working
   c. Composition

2. Metal coatings:
   a. Hot dipped
   b. Electrolytic deposition
   c. Thickness measurements

E. At this point, further tests are dependent on the information desired, the amount of material submitted for examination, the skill and experience of the examiner and the equipment available.

1. Instrumental Analyses, utilizing one or more of a variety of procedures (Neutron Activation, mass

spectrography, X ray fluorescence), used in metal cases where <u>trace elemental determination</u> is desired. Less specific and of less value for <u>major</u> alloying constituents.

2. Chemical Analyses, preferable in metal cases involving <u>major alloying constituents</u> because more accurately determines such constituents. Slower than instrumental analysis, requires knowledge of constituents in sample (test against specifications).

III. Number restoration:

The restoring of serial numbers which have been obliterated and/or altered can provide valuable assistance in proving ownership and establishing stolen character of items.

A. Principles:

1. Crystal structure:

The placement of numbers into metal by stamping, electric needle or engraving procedures physically disturbs the crystal structure of the metal beneath these numbers. As a result of this <u>physical change</u>, there are associated changes in the <u>chemical activity</u> of the metal and in its <u>magnetic properties</u>. These alterations are utilized in restoration techniques.

2. Depth of deformation:

Each procedure (stamping, electric needle, engraving) disturbs the crystal structure to a greater or lesser extent. The depth of the disturbed or deformed area is dependent on the force employed in placement of number and the overall characteristics of that particular metal.
a. Stamped numbers; most serial numbers use this procedure. In general, the disturbed metal layer extends about as deep again into the metal as the depth of the stamped number.

b. Electric needle markings; tools frequently
    marked by this method. While restorable,
    the disturbed layer is significantly less deep
    than the stamped number.
c. Engraved numbers and inscriptions; since
    engraved markings are made by cutting or
    scooping out the metal, little metal deforma-
    tion results. Because of this very shallow
    disturbed layer, such markings are very
    difficult to restore.
d. Molded markings; usually part numbers or
    pattern numbers, they are formed during the
    original casting operation which produced the
    object itself. The grain structure of the
    metal in the numbered area may be different
    from the surrounding grain structure due to
    differences in cooling rates. The possibility
    exists, therefore, that such markings may be
    restored. In any event, such numbers only
    generally identify the part without differen-
    tiating it from all similar parts.

B. Restoration capabilities:

While the depth of the original disturbed area is an
important factor, the overriding consideration is
whether the obliteration process removed only the
visible markings or was extensive enough to remove
the entire underlying disturbed area.

C. Restoration techniques:

1. Etch or chemical method. Use of a chemical
    (acid or base) to detect increased chemical
    activity of the disturbed area.

2. Electrolytic method. Employs chemical as above
    but in conjunction with an electric current.
    Current speeds operation (which is its principle
    danger).

3. Magnetic particle method. Induced current creates
    magnetic fields which are altered in area of dis-
    turbed metal. When sprayed with metal particles
    suspended in a liquid vehicle such as kerosene,

the particles are attracted to the altered areas. No surface damage is caused as in the chemical methods. Success dependent on magnetic properties of different metals.

4. Heat method. Application of heat causes those crystals which have been changed by the stamping operation to undergo structural transformation (grain recrystalization and grain growth). This causes a bulged outline of the obliterated stamping on the surface of the metal. Slight sanding of the surface after heating necessary to polish bulged metal and develop contrast. <u>Procedure is critical.</u> This method best with cast steel structures such as motor blocks.

NOTES: 1. <u>Any methods listed should be employed only by qualified personnel.</u>

2. If toolmark examination to associate specific stamps with altered numbers is desired, a cast of the alteration is made prior to restoration procedures. (See Toolmark Identification Section.)

IV. Some kinds of metallic evidence:

A. Objects at the crime scene:

1. Wire used to bind robbery victims.
   a. Lead information as to its possible source.
   b. Compositional analysis for comparison with similar wire in possession of suspect.

2. Tools at a bank burglary:
   a. Manufacturer
   b. Age of tool not determinable from rust on it.

3. Devices used to perpetrate a crime - identification of manufacturer of nails in ladder.

4. Metal fragments from timing device in a bombing:
   a. Type of mechanism, manufacturer, date of manufacture.
   b. Requirements for identification of a specific clock model.

5. Wristwatch lost by a criminal or taken from victim - owner determination through jeweler's scratch markings.

6. Piece of metal auto trim at a hit-and-run scene:
   a. Make of vehicle.
   b. The vehicle.

7. Lamp bulb from a vehicle involved in a fatal accident
   a. Condition of lights - information obtainable from both broken and unbroken bulbs.
   b. Whether brakes were applied at time of impact.

8. Metal piece which has been cut from a safe door by burning.
   a. Type of equipment used.
   b. Skill of operator.

B. Objects in possession of a suspect:

   1. Metallic materials such as wire, pipe, cable, sheet metal - association with material at crime scene.

   2. Burned metal particles on clothing - cannot associate with a particular "burn job."

   3. Weapon with an obliterated serial number - number restoration to establish ownership.

V. Selection of samples:

A. Small amounts of evidence: Send all.

B. Large amounts of evidence: Investigator must understand metallurgical capabilities in order to properly select samples.

   1. Class characteristics.

   2. Identifying characteristics.

C. Removal of samples: Must be done so as not to destroy value, such as through heat or bending.

D. Mark so as to maintain chain of custody and with consideration to size of evidence items.

INSTRUMENTAL ANALYSIS

I. Introduction

By the use of the principles and instruments of science the "vision" of all investigators can be increased. The need is present because:

A. It is difficult for unaided human eye to see details smaller than the size of an eye in a needle.

B. Eye cannot see ultraviolet, X-rays, infrared rays.

Instruments can be catagorized according to the general analytical technique that they use, such as spectroscopy - chromatography.

Spectroscopy involves the interaction between chemical matter and electromagnetic radiation wherein the matter either gains or loses energy. By observing and by measuring its intensity, chemical analyses are performed.

Electromagnetic radiation, which includes light which can been seen by the eye is a continuous spectrum with high energy radiation, such as gamma rays and X-rays, at one end, visible light in the middle and low energy radiation, such as radio and television waves at the other end.

A close examination of the general area of the spectrum occupied by visible light reveals a further division of this region into ultraviolet, visible and infrared radiation.

These are used as follows:

II. Ultraviolet energy:

A. Located beyond the violet end of the rainbow or spectrum is a bank of invisible energy known as ultraviolet. This energy, although invisible, causes many substances to emit visible light. This phenomenon is known as fluorescence.

B. Uses:

1. Detection of secret inks.

2. For the reading of invisible laundry marks.

3. Assists in preliminary search for seminal stains.

4. Marking of extortion bundles.

5. For comparison examinations of plastics, paints, lipsticks, marking pencils, paper and other fluorescent materials.

6. Assist in study of altered and erased documents.

III. Infrared energy:

A. Located beyond the red end of the rainbow or spectrum is a band of energy known as infrared.

B. Uses:

1. To photograph through haze.

2. In document examinations, to read smeared charred or deteriorated writing.

3. In the study of physical erasures.

4. To distinguish between inks, dyes and pigments that appear identical in ordinary light.

5. To read ink writing or printing originally prepared with an ink which is opaque to infrared and then obliterated with an ink transparent to infrared.

IV. Visible Energy:

A. The visible spectrum or rainbow is used for studying color and coloring agents; namely, dyes and pigments.

B. Uses:

1. Comparing dyes and coloring agents in materials such as cloth or paint.

V. Instruments utilizing radiation fall into three general types--those that utilize absorbed radiation; those that measure radiation "given off" or generated; and those that utilize the bending of radiation. A discussion of these general types follows:

A. Instruments that measure absorbed radiation

    1. Ultraviolet spectrophotometers

    2. Visible spectrophotometers

    3. Infrared spectrophotometers

    These instruments pass a narrow beam of energy through a substance to be studied. As the wave lengths of energy change the amount of energy absorbed by the substance is measured and recorded on a chart. In the case of infrared energy. The chart is a fingerprint of the organic material being studied.

    They are used in the identification and comparison of plastics, rubbers, paints, vehicles and other organic compounds.

    4. Atomic absorption

        A quantitative technique whereby elements in a sample are placed in a vapor state suitable for analysis by means of a flame. In this state they can absorb characteristic frequencies of radiation generated by hollow cathode lamps emitting the light spectrum of the element to be analyzed.

        The amount of absorption is proportional to the concentration of the element in the sample.

        This technique is used to determine concentrations of specific elements in a sample. This procedure is not used for a survey-type analysis to establish which elements may be present.

B. Instruments for measuring "given off" radiation

    1. Emission Spectrograph

        Each element, such as tin, iron, copper, when properly burned, will give off light which is characteristic of itself and different from the light produced by all other elements. Uses of this technique would include:

a. Rapid analysis of all metallic constituents in an unknown substance.

b. Detection of traces of metallic impurities in residues, such as oils, ashes, glasses or metals.

c. Testing the purity of a substance.

d. Detection of rare metals.

e. Examination of paint specimens.

2. Neutron activation analysis:

This instrumental technique utilizes artificially induced radioactivity to determine the elements within a specimen. In doing this, two factors are important:

a. Wavelength: The induced radioactivity causes each element present to emit gamma rays of specific wavelengths.

b. Half-life: That time interval required for each element in the sample to decrease the intensity of its radioactivity by one-half.

The specific wavelength emitted and the "half-life" uniquely characterize the elements present in a specimen and allow for their identification. This technique will detect and measure over half of known elements and is adaptable to a wide variety of specimens in criminal cases. The advantages of this technique are:

(1) Often nondestructive.

(2) Detects elements present at parts per billion level.

(a) Arsenic and mercury in hair and bones

(b) Barium and antimony on hand after shooting firearm.

c. Gunshot residues:

In some instances the discharge of a firearm
contaminates the shooter's hand with signifi-
cantly larger amounts of the elements antimony
and barium than would normally be found on the
hand of an individual who had not recently
fired a weapon. This contamination, if present,
results from the "blow-back" of primer residues
from the cartridge. These residues may be
removed for analysis by applying molten paraffin
to the back of the index finger, thumb and
connecting web area of the hand to a thickness of
1/16 inch and allowing it to solidify to form a
lift. Lifts should be taken from these areas on
both hands. For comparison purposes an unused
sample of this paraffin should be submitted along
with the lifts.

Although many law enforcement agencies utilize
cotton swabs moistened with 5% nitric acid
instead of paraffin lifts, it has been the
Laboratory's experience from processing such
submissions that the paraffin lift method affords
the most consistent means of removing these
residues from the hand.

In gunshot residue cases, the examiner must have
certain information in order to properly interpret
the data obtained from the analysis of the
paraffin lifts. Thus, the following general
information regarding the shooting and arrest
should be provided.

(1) Time and date of shooting.

(2) Time and date of taking lifts.

(3) Environmental conditions i.e., indoors,
     outdoors, wind conditions.

(4) Treatment afforded subject, i.e., if
     wounded, were hands washed or contaminated
     in any way during medical treatment.

(5) Activity of subject from arrest until
     specimens obtained, i.e., washing of hands
     or fingerprinting.

(6) Number of shots fired.

(7) If recovered, submit gun and cartridge case(s).

(8) Information regarding subject:

    (a) Right or left handed.

    (b) Occupation.

C. Instrument utilizing measurements of "bent" radiation

  1. X-ray diffraction

    a. An instrument used to identify and compare unknown crystalline substances. Two crystals which differ in chemical composition also differ in size and shape. Two crystals similar in size and shape will bend (diffract) X-rays in a similar manner. If the crystals are different in size and shape, they will bend (diffract) a beam of X-rays differently. The X-ray Diffraction Spectrometer records the manner in which X-rays are bent by a given crystal.

    b. Uses:

      (1) Identification of unknown crystalline material.

      (2) Identification of mixtures of crystals.

      (3) Comparisons of unknown crystals.

VI. Miscellaneous Types of Instrumentation

A. Mass spectrograph:

  1. A mass spectrograph is an instrument which ionizes a sample under examination, separates the ions according to their characteristic masses and record the spectrum.

2. Uses:

    a. Detection of trace elements present in extremely low levels in metals, glasses, ashes, and other normally inorganic materials.

    b. Analysis of unknown metallic substances.

    c. Comparison of known and questioned metallic substances.

B. Gas chromatography:

1. Essentially used as analytical method for the separation and identification of gases or liquids from complex mixtures or solutions.

2. Uses: Analysis of any organic material (both quantitative and qualitative) such as narcotics, explosives, paints, plastics, inks or petroleum products.

3. Advantages:

    a. One operation gives complete analysis of all the organic materials present in the sample for comparative tests.

    b. It can be used for solving a wide variety of analytical tasks through the analysis of volatile solids, high-boiling liquids or gases.

    c. Recording and evaluation of the analytical results are not time-consuming.

VII.   National Automotive Paint File - An Investigative Aid

A.   The file consists of paint panels received from automobile manufacturers. These paint panels are representative of the original finishes placed on automobiles at time of manufacture.

B.   Uses:

1.   To identify the year and make of car from small chip left at scene of crime.

2.   To use as reference file in all cases involving automobile paint.

VIII.   General notes to investigators:

A.   If paint samples are to be obtained from any painted surface, chip the paint off the surface rather than scrape it off. When paint is chipped off a surface, its layer structure is intact. Each layer is a point of identification. It is better to have eleven layers of paint on a questioned and known specimen than eleven layers on the questioned specimen and only the top layer in the known specimen.

B.   Be careful in the packing and marking of small paint chips and other small particles of evidence.

1.   Do not stick small paint particles on Scotch tape--remember these small particles have to be removed from the container, cleaned and packed in a small electrode.

2.   Do not put small particles in cotton. It is difficult to remove the particles from the cotton.

3.   Do not send in envelope, unless protected in paper using druggist fold.

C. If investigation develops a suspect and he has foreign stain on his hands or clothes which you believe may be associated with the scene of crime-- ask suspect where the smear or stain cam from. If possible, obtain a sample of substance suspect reports stain to have originated from for a Laboratory comparison with the questioned stain.

D. In fraud cases where specimen has to be compared with specifications, accurately state specifications.

RADIATION HAZARDS

I. Introduction:

   Radioactive materials are becoming common items through
   growth of nuclear power industry. Accidents, deaths and
   injuries resulting from handling and transportation of
   such material have been few. The future probability of
   serious accident or civilian incident requiring police
   action will, hopefully, remain small. Such statistical
   prediction will be of little comfort to those departments
   faced with a crisis of this type. Since the hazard is
   invisible, prudence dictates that a basic knowledge of
   radiation will insure intelligent action.

II. Terminology:

   A. Atoms

      Atoms are small particles of matter which have
      elemental characteristics. For example, gold and
      silver are both elements and the smallest particle
      of gold or silver which can be identified as gold
      or silver is an atom of gold or an atom of silver.

   B. Isotopes

      Isotopes are varieties of the same element which have
      the same chemical properties but have different
      nuclear structure and therefore different physical
      properties. For example, we have three isotopes of
      hydrogen; namely, Hydrogen One, Hydrogen Two and
      Hydrogen Three.

      1. Stable Isotopes are ones which are incapable of
         spontaneous change and thus not radioactive.

      2. Unstable Isotopes undergo spontaneous changes
         and emit nuclear radiations.

III. Nuclear radiations:

   The emission of energy or particles from a nucleus.

   A. Alpha particle is a positively charged particle
      emitted from a nucleus and similar to a helium
      nucleus. It has a relatively large mass with low

penetrating power and short range. Alpha particles
will usually not penetrate the skin but danger occurs
when alpha emitters are introduced into the lungs or
intestines.

B. Beta particle is a high speed negatively charged
electron emitted from a nucleus. It has little mass,
low penetrating power and short range. The more
energetic particles will penetrate the skin. Danger
is due to skin burns and internal damage if the
emitter enters the body and lodges in a body organ.

C. Gamma Ray is a unit of radiation energy similar to
X rays. These emitters can do body damage even when
located outside of the body due to their penetrating
power.

D. Neutron is a subatomic particle which has no electrical
charge and it is one of the main particles in the
nucleus.

IV. Radiation effects:

Nuclear radiations avoid detection by all our senses.
Excessive doseages represent hazards. Police activity
in or around radiation areas requires special vigilance.
Radiation hazards are normally considered as either
external or internal hazards.

A. External hazards:
Bodily damage can result from over exposure to gamma
rays even though radioactive material is outside body.
Gamma rays are external hazards.

B. Internal hazards:
Bodily damage can result if radioactive material emit-
ting alpha and beta particles contaminates our food or
the air we breath and in this manner is taken into our
bodies in excessive amounts. Alpha and beta particles
are considered internal hazards.

V. Detection equipment:

    A.   Survey meters are portable instruments designed to enable one to evaluate a particular radiation hazard. They may be designed to detect and measure alpha, beta and gamma radiation and are used for evaluation of contaminated food and water. Survey meters read either in roentgens/hour or milliroentgens/hour (1,000 milliroentgens = 1 roentgen).

    B.   Dosimeters are pocket-size instruments used to measure total gamma dosage accumulated by the person wearing the dosimeter. Some dosimeters can be read at any time by the wearer (self-reading dosimeters). Other dosimeters such as film badges are not self-reading. These latter type dosimeters are processed in a Laboratory Dosimeter readings are normally in roentgens or milliroentgens.

    C.   Significance of detection equipment readings:

        1.   Roentgen is a standard unit of measure of the energy of X ray or gamma radiation which is absorbed. Often the term milliroentgen, which is one thousandth part of a roentgen, is used.

        2.   Biological significance of roentgen:

Acute dose (roentgens)	Probable effect of total body dose
0 to 50	No obvious effect, except possibly minor blood changes.
80 to 120	Vomiting and nausea for about 1 day in 5 to 10 percent of exposed personnel. Fatigue but no serious disability.
130 to 170	Vomiting and nausea for about 1 day, followed by other symptoms of radiation sickness in about 25 percent of personnel. No deaths anticipated.

72

180 to 220	Vomiting and nausea for about 1 day, followed by other symptoms of radiation sickness in about 50 percent of personnel. No deaths anticipated.
270 to 330	Vomiting and nausea in nearly all personnel on first day, followed by other symptoms of radiation sickness. About 20 percent deaths within 2 to 6 weeks after exposure; survivors convalescent for about 6 months.
400 to 500	Vomiting and nausea in all personnel on first day, followed by other symptoms of radiation sickness. About 50 percent deaths within 1 month; survivors convalescent for about 6 months.
550 to 750	Vomiting and nausea in all personnel within 4 hours from exposure, followed by other symptoms of radiation sickness. Up to 100 percent deaths ; few survivors convalescent for about 6 months.
1000	Vomiting and nausea in all personnel within 1 to 2 hours. Probably no survivors from radiation sickness.
5000	Incapacitation almost immediately. All personnel will be fatalities within 1 week.

VI. Factors concerning protection:

A. If all containers of radioactive material are sealed or closed and are <u>intact</u> it is unlikely that radio-active hazards are associated with the incident. Efforts should be made to protect the integrity of the containers during essential rescue, salvage and clean-up operations.

B. If radioactive isotopes are loosed from container or liberated by a handling accident the following factors should be understood.

   1. Distance. The distance between individuals and the isotope source appreciably decreases radiation intensity. In most cases, for example, the distance of 2 feet from the source will decrease the radiation to one-quarter its value at 1 foot; a distance of 10 feet from the source will decrease the radiation to one-hundredth its value at 1 foot.

   2. Time. The time one spends in the radiation field should be kept to an absolute minimum. A 2-hour exposure in a radiation field will be twice as large as a 1-hour exposure.

   3. Shielding. Dense materials such as steel, concrete and dirt between the individual and the source can cut down the intensity of gamma radiation. Most gamma-emitting radioisotopes emit radiation of less than one million electron volts. Generally, the radiation may be cut in half by 1½ inches of steel, 4½ inches of concrete, 7½ inches of earth, or 10 inches of water.

   4. Containment. Restriction of the radioisotopes to a limited area will help to establish boundaries for the hazard. Efforts should be made to keep the radioisotope from scattering. If there is a fire associated with an incident, high pressure hoses might break open containers and widely distribute the radioisotopes. Vehicles and individuals repeatedly entering the area could track away any radioisotopes from incidents involving spills of radioactive materials. Such travel should be limited to that which is absolutely necessary.

C.   External or internal hazards, or both, can be present whenever radioactive materials are found. If it is not known what the hazards are, assume both to be present. To protect against internal hazards personnel should wear breathing masks or some type of filter system over the nose or mouth. If possible, all personnel should be kept upwind from the scene of the incident and all smoking and eating should be prohibited in the restricted area. Personnel entering the area where there is radioactive dust should be wearing disposable or washable outer clothing.

VII. Emergency procedures for accident:

A.   Keep all but rescue personnel away from immediate accident scene.

B.   Report accident immediately to the Energy Research and Development Administration (ERDA) or military base, whichever is appropriate.

C.   Keep sightseers away - 500 yards or more, if possible.

D.   Stay out of smoke or vapors if fire is associated with accident.

E.   Hold people who may have been exposed to contamination in an area for appropriate examination by emergency personnel.

F.   Do not fight fires involving explosives except under direction of an expert.

G.   Do not permit the taking of souvenirs.

H.   Keep unauthorized personnel from entering the scene.

EXPLOSIVES

I. Introduction:

    A. Types of explosions:

        1. <u>Mechanical</u> - illustrated by the gradual buildup of
            pressure in a steam boiler or pressure cooker. If
            the boiler or pressure cooker is not equipped with
            some type of safety valve, the mounting steam pres-
            sure will eventually reach a point when it will
            overcome the structural resistance of its container
            and an explosion will occur.

        2. <u>Atomic</u> - may be induced by either fission (the
            splitting of the nucleus of atoms) or fusion (the
            joining together under great force of the nuclei
            of atoms).

        3. <u>Chemical</u> - the rapid conversion of a solid or liq-
            uid explosive compound into gases having a much
            greater volume than the substances from which they
            are generated. The entire conversion process takes
            only a fraction of a second and is accompanied by
            shock, heat and loud noise. All explosives manu-
            factured by man are chemical explosives with the
            exception of atomic explosives. Chemical explosions
            are the type of most importance to law enforcement.

    B. Classification of explosives:

        1. Low explosives - rate of change to gaseous state
            is relatively slow - deflagration reaction. Included
            would be:
            a. Black powder
            b. Smokeless powder

        2. High explosives - rate of change to gaseous state
            is extremely rapid - detonation reaction. Included
            would be:
            a. Commercial dynamites
            b. Military explosives such as TNT or C4

II. Effects of an explosion:

    A. Blast pressure effect

        1. Positive pressure phase

2. Negative pressure phase

B. Fragmentation effect

C. Incendiary thermal effect

III. Blasting accessories:

A. Safety fuse

B. Detonating cord

C. Blasting caps

D. Fuse lighters

E. Blasting machines

F. Initiating devices

IV. Handling of bombs:

A. <u>Don't</u>, unless qualified.

B. Have available names of nearest qualified disposal experts in event suspected bomb <u>must</u> be handled.

C. Suggested list of steps to follow upon discovery:

1. Clear area.
2. Get services of explosives expert.
3. Don't move or touch anything connected with it.
4. Post guards outside danger area.
5. Shut off power, fuel, electric and gas services.
6. Remove flammable material.
7. Notify fire and rescue squads.
8. Arrange for medical aid to stand by.

V. Disposition of explosives: should be handled only by a person familiar with such materials and trained in proper disposal techniques.

BOMB SCENE SEARCHES

This section is to assist in preparing for supervising and evaluating activity connected with the scene of a bombing. Topics covered are not meant to be all-inclusive. No attempt has been made to comment on many aspects of the bombing investigation.

I. Purpose of crime scene investigation: To determine what happened and why it happened:

    A. Result of bomb explosion:

        1. Identify bomber:
            a. If survived, sufficient evidence to prosecute.
            b. If died in explosion, identify bomber, determine what was used and how.

        2. Provide information to public.

    B. Accidental explosion:

        1. Cause

        2. Provide pertinent information to public.

II. Plan of action: Each agency should have a plan of action, preferably in writing, for conducting the bombing investigation

    A. No universal plan. Formulate own plan to fit particular needs.

    B. Assignment of personnel and fixing responsibility.

    C. One man in overall charge of investigation.

    D. One man in overall charge of crime scene. Reports directly to official in overall charge of investigation.

    E. Periodic review and updating of plan. BE PREPARED - HAVE A PLAN.

III. Bomb scene specialist: Have a specialist trained in handling and processing bomb scenes or arrangements made for obtaining such an individual. Although basic principles of conducting a crime scene apply, specialized knowledge is necessary:

A. Thorough knowledge of explosives, improvised explosive devices and damage produced by explosive charges.

B. Oriented toward physical evidence and must be aware of types of examinations a Laboratory can conduct. Improperly collected evidence of limited or no value.

C. Need not be a qualified bomb disposal specialist; however, such training can be invaluable relative to problems which may arise at the scene.

IV. Equipment: Debris and material at the scene must be moved. Have necessary equipment or arrangements made for promptly obtaining same. Although the equipment needed <u>at the scene</u> varies, **the** following have been used:

A. Hand tools: Shovels, rakes, brooms, boltcutters, wire cutters, sledgehammer, hammer, screwdrivers, wrenches, chisels, hacksaw, magnet, flashlights, knife, 50' measuring tape, traffic wheel measuring device.

B. Other light equipment: Screens for sifting debris, wheelbarrows, metal trash cans, power saw, cutting torch equipment, ladders, portable lighting equipment, metal detector, large plastic sheets, photographic equipment, parachute harness with related rope and pulleys.

C. Heavy equipment: Truck, front-end loader, bulldozer, crane, shoring materials.

D. Personal equipment: Hard hats, safety goggles, gloves - work and rubber types, foul weather clothing, coveralls, work shoes.

E. Usual crime scene kit.

F. Vehicles: If target is vehicle, have identical vehicle available at scene.

V. Command post: Consider establishing a command post at the scene of a large bombing which may require days or weeks to complete:

   A. Handling of inquiries and problems:

       1. Coordinating own efforts

       2. Press inquiries

       3. Coordinating efforts of other agency representatives

       4. Public:
           a. Sightseers
           b. Persons associated with scene
           c. Relatives of victims

   B. Coordination of efforts at scene and collateral investigations.

VI. Safety: Evaluate safety conditions at outset of crime scene activity and on a continuing basis throughout crime scene operation:

   A. Possibility of second bomb in area and possibility of second bomb "jammed" by debris.

   B. Possibility of live explosives being in the debris.

   C. Crowds and nearby residents.

   D. Personnel involved in processing crime scene.

VII. Protection of crime scene: This major problem commences immediately following the explosion and is complicated by the variety of personnel who will respond:

   A. Firemen

   B. Rescue squad

   C. Utility personnel

   D. Sightseers

   E. Victims or individuals with personal interest in property

VIII. Chain of custody: This vital aspect of collecting evidence
      is often overlooked. Valuable evidence may not be admissible
      if a proper chain of custody cannot be established.

      A. One man in charge of all evidence.

      B. Evidence properly identified.

      C. Too many collectors.

IX.   Photographic presentation of scene: A photographic presen-
      tation of the scene should be prepared. Photographs should
      be made immediately following explosion, periodically during
      processing of the scene and at completion of crime scene
      activity. (See appropriate material, Law Enforcement
      Photography, Parts II, B and C)

      A. Coordinate photographs with diagram, blueprint or map.

      B. Consider advisability of aerial photographs.

      C. Properly identified.

X.   Theory of conducting crime scene: A crime scene search
      must be conducted on the theory that everything at the scene
      prior to the explosion is still in existence unless it has
      been vaporized by the explosion. Locating and identifying
      items is the problem. The often-used statement that so much
      is destroyed by the explosion that the cause must remain
      unknown is rarely true:

      A. Mental attitude of searchers:

          1. Interest

          2. Training

          3. Experience

      B. Don't stop after finding few items.

      C. Tendency to concentrate only on physical evidence which
          may represent bomb. Can result in overlooking valuable
          evidence such as fingerprints, tire tread impressions or
          shoe prints.

XI. Search techniques: The method of searching varies depending on uncontrollable factors. Generally, commence at site of explosion and work outward:

A. Well-organized, thorough and careful search usually prevents necessity of second search. Have secure "dump" area for debris in event second search necessary.

B. Evidence has been found several blocks from sites of large explosions. Often tendency not to search sufficient distance from site of explosion.

C. Following technique for searching large area using line of searchers found to be satisfactory:

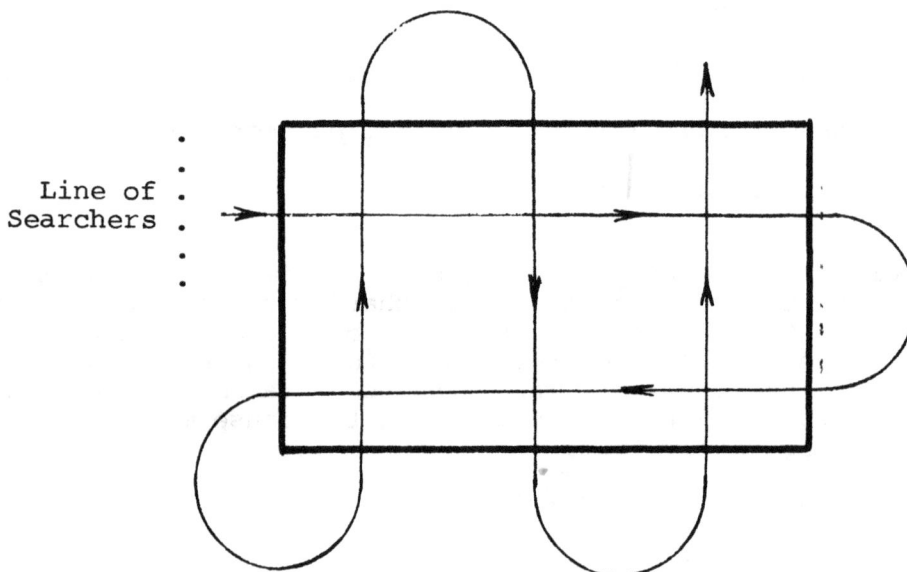

Crime scene specialist should follow line of searchers to evaluate items found, control searchers, furnish guidance. If second search desirable, rotate positions of searchers.

D. Possible flight paths of bomb components to prevent needless searching.

E. Search trees, shrubbery, the roofs, ledges and gutters of buildings, telephone poles.

F. Sift small debris. Sift through ¼" hardware cloth onto insect-type screen wire.

G. Retain all items foreign to scene and items you cannot identify. Obtain assistance of individual familiar with target.

H. Crater: If in earth, obtain soil samples from perimeter of crater and from sides and bottom of crater. Dig into substrata. If in other material, obtain similar samples.

XII. The "dead can talk." X-ray bodies of victims in close proximity to site of explosion and have possible evidence removed. Retain clothing which may contain explosive residues

XIII. Amount of explosive used: Due to various factors, the exact amount of explosive used cannot be determined based on an evaluation of damage at the scene.

XIV. Evidence: Principal evidence leading to identification of bomber and successful prosecution may be present at scene:

A. Safety fuse:

1. Manufacturer

2. Brand and burning rate

3. Possibility of end match

B. Detonating cord:

1. Manufacturer

2. Brand

C. Electric blasting caps:

1. Manufacturer

2. Type

3. Leg wire:
   a. Manufacturer
   b. Type of blasting cap

D. Nonelectric blasting caps: Manufacturer

E. Dynamite wrappers:

1. Manufacturer and brand

2. Date-plant-shift code

3. Determine diameter of cartridge before removing wrapper

F. Clock and timing devices:

1. Reference collection - disassembled devices

2. Make and model

3. Date of manufacture

4. How device altered

G. Batteries:

1. Reference collection - disassembled batteries

2. Manufacturer

3. Type and manufacturer's code

H. Electronic or electric components: Manufacturer

I. Miscellaneous:

1. Fingerprints
2. Document

3. Tire tread impressions
4. Shoe prints
5. Hair and fiber
6. Soil
7. Blood
8. Instrumental
9. Tape
10. Toolmarks
11. Engineering
12. Metallurgy

J. Identification of particular explosive used:

1. Unconsumed explosives.
2. Portions of explosive container:
   a. Dynamite wrapper.
   b. Metal end cap from TNT block: plastic end cap of C4 block.
   c. Fragments from binary explosive containers.
3. Residues:
   a. Obtain items adjacent to or in close proximity of bomb.
   b. Place in airtight containers.

K. Live explosives:

1. Don't handle unless qualified.
2. Don't bring to unauthorized area.
3. If samples to be submitted to a Laboratory, contact for instructions.
4. Destruction following examination.

L. Live bombs:

Life and safety of bomb disposal personnel has priority over obtaining of evidence. Insure such personnel cognizant value of evidence. (Don't use 2 lbs. C4 in Rendering Safe Procedure (RSP) if ¼ lb. will suffice.)

LAW ENFORCEMENT PHOTOGRAPHY

I. Introduction:

   Photography must be considered essential to every law
   enforcement activity. To make photography pay the
   greatest rewards, proper equipment and trained personnel
   for this purpose must be available. Proper recognition
   of the values of photography to law enforcement will
   result in a service that will not only pay for itself
   but will provide dividends. Crime and accident scenes,
   individual items of evidence, the commission of a crime; all
   can be accurately recorded, retained and presented through
   photographs. The many uses of law enforcement photography
   from training and public relations to pictorial court
   presentations are indispensable to the modern law enforcement department. The purpose of this discussion is to
   examine some of the important functions of photography to
   law enforcement and to consider the means of attaining
   those functions together with some of the problems
   involved.

II. Functions:

   A. Identification records:

      1. Personal identification:
         a. Prisoner photographs
         b. Suspects
         c. Missing persons
         d. Drivers licenses
         e. Firearms
         f. Itinerant peddlers
         g. Bartenders
         h. Taxi drivers

      2. Files:
         a. Lost property
         b. Fraudulent checks
         c. Anonymous letters

   B. Recording the crime or accident scene:

      1. Exteriors:
         a. Establish location of scene by photograph
             from distance which will include a landmark.

        b. Medium distance photographs to record relative
            positions of closely related items of evidence.
        c. Close-up photographs of individual items of
            evidence.

    2. Interiors:
        a. Establish location of building through
            photographs.
        b. Photographs of rooms and other interior areas
            from typical observation points using wide
            angle lens when necessary to show relative
            positions of all items within area.
        c. Medium distance photographs showing relative
            positions of closely related items of evidence.
        d. Close-up photographs of individual items of
            evidence.

C. Evidence photography:

    1. At scene:
        a. Record condition of individual items of
            evidence before recovery.
        b. Reproduce shoe, tire, and similar impressions
            which can be recorded in no other way or
            prior to attempts to lift or cast.

    2. At Headquarters:
        a. Further detailed photograph of individual
            items of evidence, especially if evidence
            may deteriorate or become altered.
        b. Recording latent fingerprints.
        c. Copy photography of documents and related
            materials.

    3. In the Laboratory:
        a. Recording condition of individual items of
            evidence prior to any alterations.
        b. Recording results of examinations.
        c. Recording evidence for further examinations
            from photographs.
        d. Producing evidence not normally visible.

D. Recording the criminal and the crime:

    1. Surveillance photography

         a. Still photographs for identification photo-
             graphs of individuals.
         b. Movies for record of activity.

     2. Camera traps - camera controlled and/or activated
         by remote means.

     3. Confessions

     4. Re-enactments

     5. Drunken-driver tests

  E. Court presentation:

     1. Admissibility:

        Photographs must be undistorted, true and faithful
        reproductions.

     2. Photograph serves as an aid to a witness:
         a. Not ordinarily necessary for photographer to
             testify, but if called upon, he should have
             record of full details regarding camera used,
             lighting, film and exposures.
         b. Charts and overlays.
         c. Use to demonstrate evidentiary points.

III. In summary, an efficient photographic department can be an
    economic asset to any law enforcement agency by:

  A. Acting as a crime deterrent through aid given to successful
     prosecutions.

  B. Savings of investigators' time as an adjunct to note
     taking and chart making.

  C. Savings of prosecutors' and witnesses' time (including
     law enforcement officers) in preparations for trial.

  D. Savings of court time, including judge, lawyers, witnesses
     and jurors by simplification and clarification of testi-
     mony.

DOCUMENT EXAMINATION

I. Introduction:

   A. Definition:

      Document examinations consist for the most part of a side-by-side comparison of handwriting, typewriting and other written or printed matter from an identification standpoint.

   B. Conclusions are positive and reliable when examinations conducted by competent experts.

   C. Age or sex in handwriting cannot be determined with certainty.

   D. Consideration should always be given to treating documents for latent fingerprints. (Done after evidence is photographed and document examination is completed.)

II. The physical identification of questioned documents:

   A. Initial and date each document unless legal aspects or good judgment dictates otherwise.

   B. If documents should not be initialed:

      1. Place in individual clear plastic envelopes, along with a slip of paper showing initials, date and other pertinent data.

      2. Place in other suitable individual envelopes, on the outside of which show initials, date and other pertinent data.

II. Why the original evidence itself rather than photocopies should be submitted:

A. Many types of examinations can be made only on the original evidence, for example:

1. Most types of forgeries

2. Certain kinds of typewriting

3. Checkwriter impressions or notary seals.

B. The originals are needed for making court exhibits.

C. Photographic copies of good quality may be satisfactory for a Laboratory examination in lieu of the originals.

D. In no case should inability to forward the originals constitute a valid reason for not requesting a Laboratory examination.

E. Photocopies are satisfactory for check file searches.

IV. The letter of transmittal as related to document cases:

A. List the evidence, clearly distinguishing between the questioned and known.

B. State exactly what examinations are desired.

C. State whether the questioned material should be treated for latent fingerprints.

D. State exactly how the known samples were obtained.

E. In check cases, furnish a physical description of the subject, if available.

F. Note any effort by subject to disguise writing or any personal characteristics, such as nervousness.

G. Place evidence in envelope and seal, then attach to letter of transmittal and place in large envelope for shipment.

90

V. The elements of a Laboratory report:

    A. A summary of the results of the examination.

    B. Reason for "no conclusion" reports:

        1. Disguise (definite conclusion often impossible).

        2. Limited questioned material.

        3. Borderline cases -- even though ample quantities of both questioned and known samples are available, the writing is not sufficiently characteristic.

        4. Inadequate known material.

        5. Lack of contemporaneous standards (where long interval of time exists).

    C. Suggestions made by examiner to assist investigator.

    D. Status of evidence - when it may be expected back or if retained.

VI. Obtaining known handwriting samples:

REPRODUCE THE ORIGINAL CONDITIONS AS NEARLY AS POSSIBLE.

    A. Obtain samples from dictation until it is believed normal writing has been produced (the number of samples necessary cannot be determined in advance).

    B. Do not allow the suspect to see either the original document in question or a photograph thereof.

    C. Remove each sample from the sight of the writer as soon as it is completed.

    D. Do not give instructions in spelling, punctuation or arrangement.

    E. Use the same writing media, such as type and size of paper, writing instruments, printed forms such as checks or notes.

F. Obtain the full text of the questioned writing in word-for-word order at least once, if possible. Signatures and less extensive writing should be prepared several times, each time on a different piece of paper Obscene passages or proper nouns may be omitted from the dictation.

G. In forgery cases the Laboratory should also be furnished with genuine signatures of the person whose name is forged.

H. Obtain samples with both the right and left hands.

I. Obtain samples written rapidly, slowly, and at varied slants.

J. Obtain samples of supplementary writings.

K. Writer should initial each page.

L. Witness each sample on the back, never on the front.

M. If readily available, samples of normal undictated writing should be obtained, such as applications for employment, social or business correspondence, school papers, written at approximately the same dates as the questioned writing.

II. Obtaining known typewriting samples:

A. Obtain a full word-for-word text of the message in question using as nearly as possible the same degree of touch as on questioned.

B. Obtain complete keyboard, i.e., all letters, numerals, symbols.

C. Obtain pertinent identifying data regarding typewriter make, model, serial, date sample taken and by whom, place where located, who owns or has access to machine

D. Obtain data, if available, regarding when machine was last serviced or repaired.

E. Properly witness each sample (initial and date on reverse side).

92

F. If typewriter is equipped with paper-type ("one-time") ribbon, remove used portion and submit to Laboratory whenever available.

G. If new cloth ribbon is used on typewriter, consider removing it and submitting to Laboratory. Also obtain stencil sample (use carbon paper in place of ribbon) of at least complete keyboard.

H. If typewriter is not equipped with ribbon or ribbon is not readily available, samples may be taken by substituting carbon paper for ribbon (stencil sample).

    NOTE: Stencil sample gives very clear impression of type faces.

VIII. Forgery examinations:

A. Traced (try to locate pattern or master signature from which traced).

B. Simulated or copied (include samples of genuine signatures to determine extent of simulation).

C. Freehand (forger has no knowledge of how genuine signature looks).

IX. Standard reference files:

A. Typewriting standards

B. Watermark standards

C. Safety paper

D. Checkwriters

E. Shoe print and tire tread

X. Files of questioned material:

    A. National Fraudulent Check File

    B. Anonymous Letter File

    C. Bank Robbery Note File

XI. Summary of all types of document examinations:

    A. Handwriting (script).

    B. Hand printing or hand lettering.

    C. Forgeries (usually difficult to identify writer of tracings or simulations since these are tracings or copies of genuine writings of another person and thus do not reflect the normal handwriting characteristics of the writer).

    D. Typewriting (new machines difficult to identify).

    E. Paper (definite identification seldom possible); watermarks (dating techniques); cut and torn edges.

    F. Inks (ordinarily writing fluids, ball-point, printing).

    G. Writing instruments (pencils, pens, crayons, ball-point pens).

    H. Checkwriters (difficult to identify).

    I. Printing and other duplication processes.

    J. Indented writing (do not fold or crease).

    K. Obliterated or eradicated writing (advise whether chemical methods may be applied).

    L. Used carbon paper (do not fold or crease).

    M. Burned or charred paper (ship between layers of cotton in a strong box).

SHOE PRINT AND TIRE TREAD EVIDENCE

I.   Methods of collecting physical evidence:

    A.   Retain original when possible and practical.

    B.   Photographs

    C.   Casts (soil, sand, snow).

    D.   Lifts (from hard, smooth surfaces).

II. Photography at crime scene - <u>photographs should supplement casts and lifts</u>:

    A.   Photograph general crime scene area.

    B.   Photograph showing positions of individual items of evidence within crime scene area.

    C.   Evidence photographs of shoe prints and tire tread impressions for Laboratory use:

        1.   Use camera on tripod. Polaroid <u>not</u> recommended.

        2.   Place ruler and identification label beside impression.

        3.   Set camera directly over impression and focus so impression fills negative.

        4.   Expose while holding light source (flash gun) to one side and low.

        5.   Take second photograph with light rotated through 90° horizontally.

III. Casts - should always be made where applicable:

    NOTE: Many different substances can be used for casting purposes such as silicone rubber products, commercial products such as Castone, and flowers of sulphur for snow. Plaster of Paris is usually recommended as it is relatively inexpensive and usually more readily available.

A. Produces <u>positive</u> impression of object causing original
    questioned impression. Cast all available shoe impres-
    sions and the entire circumferences of all tires (in
    sections), if practical.

B. Materials:

    1. Good grade of plaster (plaster without fiber content)
        or other casting material with which investigator
        is familiar.

    2. Container for mixing.

    3. Water for plaster casts.

    4. Sticks, twigs or wire for re-enforcement of plaster
        casts.

    5. Paddle for stirring.

    6. Strips of wood or metal for form around impression.

    7. Spray gun, plastic spray or something similar may
        be needed for problem impressions such as those in
        loose dirt or sand.

    8. Flowers of sulphur can be used for impressions in
        snow. These casts are brittle and should be "backed"
        with a stronger material such as Plaster of Paris.
        Heat crystals in double boiler to liquid form, let
        cool till film appears on surface, pour gently into
        impression.

C. Preparation of impression:

    1. Clean out <u>loose</u> material carefully - do not disturb
        impression.

    2. Plastic spray or hair spray may be used to fix
        problem impressions such as those in sand or loose
        dirt. Use of spray should be limited to those
        with proper experience. Improperly used, sprays
        may cause loss in detail neccesary for minute com-
        parison purposes. Some success has been noted with
        the use of fine water spray in connection with sand
        impressions.

96

3. Forms around impressions to confine plaster and improve appearance of casts.

D. Preparation of Plaster of Paris mixture:

1. Start with approximately enough water to fill impression.
2. Sprinkle plaster into water; stir continually until mixture is about consistency of thin pancake batter.
3. Pour immediately - do not break flow before entire surface is covered - pour gently to avoid "washing away" impression.
4. Place re-enforcements after pouring plaster approximately ½ inch thick.
5. Renew pouring until cast is 1 to 1½ inches thick.
6. Scratch date, initials and other pertinent information into back of cast while still relatively soft.
7. Remove only loose material from face of cast when lifted. Improper cleaning before cast cures can damage detail of surface impression.
8. Cast is very fragile - must be handled carefully, especially for mailing. <u>Do</u> <u>not place casts</u> <u>in plastic</u> <u>bags</u>. Dry casts thoroughly before shipping.
9. If casts are sent through mails, wrap in manner to avoid breakage during shipment.
10. When occasion arises for you to make a cast and if you have not previously made any such casts, it is suggested that you make an impression with your own shoe and practice making a cast before you work with the original evidence. Casts and lifts destroy the questioned impressions when they are removed and care should be taken to insure perfect reproductions.

IV. Impressions on firm surfaces:

A. Search suspect areas with flashlight and darken area if possible. Direct the beam of light parallel to suspect surfaces.

B. Photograph:

Evidence photograph should be made by method described in Part II. Hold light source as close to floor as possible for side lighting effect.

C. Retain original evidence, if possible, to send to Lab-
    oratory. Protect impressions so they will not rub off
    in handling.

D. Lift impression if original evidence cannot be retained.

    1. Use large pieces of fingerprint lifting tape and
        lift print - do not dust or otherwise treat impression
        Start tape at one edge and roll over impression
        attempting to keep out air bubbles.
    2. Photographic film - gelatin on film when moistened
        forms excellent surface for lifting impressions:
        a. Clear film made by fixing and washing. Black
            film made by exposing, developing, fixing and
            washing.
        b. Film should be placed in water, wiped off and
            dried until tacky.
        c. The tacky film should be applied to impression
            with squeegee (scraper or roller) from one edge
            using care to avoid air bubbles.
    3. Protect lifted impressions so they will not be
        destroyed or "erased" during handling or shipping.

V. Laboratory examinations:

    A. Files for determination of possible manufacturer of shoe
        or tire that made a particular questioned impression:

        1. Shoe Print File: Contains photographs of designs used
            in soles and heels made by major manufacturers in U. S
        2. Tire Tread File: contains blueprints, drawings or
            photographs of tire tread patterns furnished by tire
            manufacturers.

    B. Comparison of cast, photograph or lift made from a
        questioned impression with a tire or shoe. Positive
        identification depends on detail reproduced from
        original impression and presence of identifying defects
        as a result of wear.

CRYPTANALYSIS - GAMBLING - TRANSLATION SECTION

This section is responsible for the examination of codes and ciphers, i.e., developing communications intelligence through cryptanalysis; for the preparation, implementation and material support of code and cipher systems used for the Bureau's communications security; for translation of foreign language materials; and for anaylsis of gambling paraphernalia.

I. Cryptanalysis Unit

The Cryptanalysis Unit has two primary responsibilities, Communications Security and Communications Intelligence.

Communications Security. This unit is responsible for the preparation and/or obtaining of cryptomaterials for the Bureau's own communications. This responsibility includes training in the use of certain equipments, the clearance of personnel for cryptoaccess and the accountability of the material through Communications Security Custodians in the Field.

Communications Intelligence. Communications Intelligence covers a broad spectrum of activity. The scope of this activity includes, but is not necessarily restricted to

A. Miscellaneous codes and ciphers.

B. Physical material of any kind, the significance of which is unknown or obscure. This could include:

   1. Normal script so badly written as not to be understandable.

   2. Physical objects with marks or designs which might contain intelligible information.

   3. Apparent mathematical formulas or calculations which do not appear to have any logical forms or intent.

   4. Computer printouts or the like.

   5. Maps, diagrams, etc., the intent of which is unknown.

6. Any kind of written material, the meaning or intent of which is obscure.

C. Enciphered telephone numbers or addresses.

D. Authorship Identification, with either aural or written material.

    1. Determination as to whether two (or more) items were prepared by the same person.

    2. Determination of background information on the author; accent, education, ethnic characteristics, etc.

    3. Analysis includes
       a. Grammatical usage, word and phrase selection and incorrect usage and spelling.
       b. Mathematical analysis of certain pertinent ratios.

E. General mathematical analysis.

    1. Manifestations of probability and chance.

    2. Analysis of documents, etc., (such as tachographs) which requires mathematical manipulations.

Because of the unique nature of cryptanalytically oriented examinations, whenever possible, as much information as available should be furnished. As a minimum, when known, this should include, but not be restricted to:

A. Any information as to the intent of the material submitted.

B. Complete background information as pertinent.

C. Any foreign languages possibly involved.

D. Special training the subject may have had that could be of interest.

It should be noted that material for cryptanalytic examination could be in almost any format, such as:

A. Normal English letters.

100

B. Numbers (including Arabic numerals).

C. Symbols (including Chinese characters).

D. Dots or any other graphical manifestation (including musical notations).

II. Gambling Unit:

The Gambling Unit has the capability to make technical examinations of physical evidence and monitored telephone intercepts in matters relating to numbers (numbers-pool, policy, Bolita, Cuba), sports events (football, baseball, basketball, horse racing), lottery tickets, tip boards, playing cards, dice and related gambling matters; and can furnish competent experts to testify in court relative to this evidence. Generally, expert testimony will not be furnished on purely hypothetical matters or general gambling procedures where no evidence was made available for Laboratory examination.

III. Federal Gambling Statutes:

A. Interstate Transmission of Wagering Information.

B. Interstate Transportation of Wagering Paraphernalia.

C. Interstate Transportation of Gambling Devices.

D. Interstate Transportation in Aid of Racketeering-Gambling.

E. Interstate Transportation of Lottery Tickets.

F. Illegal Gambling Business (IGB) - requiring violation of State law, five or more persons involved in the operation who manage, supervise, direct, conduct, own or finance rather than mere bettors, and either more than 30 days continuous operation or at least $2,000 in any one day of wagering. Illegal for a person under color of office to conspire with persons engaged in gambling (as defined in IGB statute) to thwart enforcement of local gambling laws.

IV. Types of documentary evidence:

A. Wagering Slips - need to establish if the wagers are personal wagers or wagers of different bettors. Used in determining volume of wagering.

B. Summaries of wagering slips or tallies, showing wagers of numerous individuals or accounts; charting of wagers, systematically done to determine volume of wagering on various events.

C. Accounting and financial records or bottom sheets showing numerous accounts, (sometimes code-designated), amounts and/or commissions paid to writers.

D. Related paraphernalia - sports schedules or line sheets, sports records materials, dream books, cut cards, parlay manuals, conversion charts, scratch sheets, racing forms

V. Numbers wagering - sometimes called policy, Bolita, Cuba; Puerto Rico, stocks and bonds, Chicago Wheel, or lottery:

A. Winning number usually is two or three digits.

B. Methods of determining winning number:

1. From combined pari-mutuel totals of horse races.

2. From total handle of a race track.

3. From post positions or individual number of horses or dogs.

4. Stocks and bonds volumes or statistics.

5. Treasury and Clearing House balances.

6. Puerto Rican National Lottery Number.

7. Drawings.

C. Types of wagers:

1. Straight bets on the 2- or 3-digit number.

2. Combination, box, bird-cage bets on each of the 3 or 6 ways the 3-digit number can be arranged.

3. Single and double action - bets on only 1 or 2 of the digits of a 2- or 3-digit number.

D. Specialized vocabulary:

1. Cut numbers - numbers on which normal odds are cut to discourage wagering.

2. Hits - winning bets.

3. Overlooks - winning numbers overlooked in original tabulations.

4. Keep-ins, steadies, weeklies, walls - bets for multiple days or until notified to cancel the bet.

5. Layoff number is re-bet - when volume of betting on a number is too large.

6. Tapes or ribbons - adding machine tapes used to calculate wagering or summarize writers' accounts.

E. Payoff ratios - usually from 400 for 1 to 600 for 1, occasionally less a bonus to a writer, usually from 100 for 1 to 400 for 1 in cut numbers, around 60 for 1 to 70 for 1 for 2-digit numbers; around 6 for 1 to 8 for 1 for single digits.

F. Organizational structure:

1. Bets given to a writer, sometimes bettor receiving carbon of the bet, sometimes by telephone.

2. Bets from writers collected by pick-up men, collectors or runners and transmitted to office or bank. Sometimes work relayed by telephone instead.

3. Large organizations may use several banks or controllers.

4. Bets tabulated by bank, charted to determine necessity for lay-off, winning numbers determined and pay-off to writers arranged.

VI. Horse racing:

A. Pari-mutuel system:

Money wagered on each race for win, place and show put in separate pools from which is taken a percentage for Federal and State taxes and track operational expenses. Remainder of pool divided among winning wagers to determine payoff. "Breakage" means tracks pay off in next lowest even ten cents. If payoff should be $2.29, breakage rule means track only pays off $2.20, meaning a maximum additional track profit of nineteen cents for each $2.00 wagered. Overall, approximately 20% is removed from the average pool.

B. Pay-off by bookmakers:

1. Maximum pay-off is at track odds, thus giving bookmaker advantage of about 20% in vigorish.

103

599-243 O - 75 - 8

2. Bookmaker also uses limitations on pay-offs and usually does not pay off more than 50 - 1 on daily double, exacta, perfecta or quinella bets and limits on win - place - show betting of 20 - 1, 10 - 1 and 5 - 1 or 15 - 1, 8 - 1 and 5 - 1.

C. Types of wagers:

1. Straight - win (first place only), place (first or second place), show (first, second or third place).

2. Combination or across the board - equal amounts to win, place and show.

3. Daily double, winners of both first and second races - one ticket.

4. Quinella - first and second place horses in either order in designated races - one ticket.

5. Exacta and perfecta - first and second horses in that order in designated race - one ticket.

6. Trizacta and trifecta - first, second and third horses in that order in designated race - one ticket.

7. Superfecta - first four horses, in exact order, in designated race - one ticket.

8. Wheels - bets coupling one horse with all of the other horses in another race - often used in daily doubles.

9. Parlays - two or more horses in different races, each horse must win if a "win parlay." Effect is for all winnings on first horse to be re-bet on second and succeeding horses.

10. Round Robin or bird cage - series of all separate two-horse parlays that can be arranged from three or more horses.

11. "If" bets - certain amount of money bet on first horse and, if he wins, certain amount of those winnings bet on second horse.

12. If-and-reverse bets - same as "if" bet except change the order of the horses in the reverse.

D.   Lay-off - used to preclude large losses - either done
     by a re-bet with another bookmaker or by having some-
     one at the track making re-bet (sometimes referred to
     as come-back bets).

E.   Special terms:

     1.   Time bet - bookmaker records time that bet was
          placed in event race has already commenced.

     2.   Scratch sheet - printed sheet showing post times,
          horses, jockeys, weights, morning line at certain
          tracks, horses that are "scratched" or originally
          scheduled to run but were withdrawn, post position,
          handicap position, etc.

     3.   Field - all horses over 12 coupled with 12th horse
          as if one horse.

     4.   Past posting - placing a bet after the race has
          commenced.

     5.   Entry - two or more horses owned by same owner
          or using same trainer, bet as if one horse.

VII. Sports Events:

A.   Football:

     1.   Line or anticipated point spread on a game used
          as a handicap. Line distributed nationally and
          obtained by bookmaker in order to learn of injuries
          or other unpublicized factors affecting the game.
          Also, obtained nationally so that all bookmakers
          originally use same line.

     2.   Line changes - line primarily altered in order to
          encourage betting on one side, thus tending towards
          a more favorable balance of wagers from the book-
          maker's standpoint.

     3.   Vigorish or juice - bettor puts up 10% (sometimes
          20%) more than bookmaker. Thus, bookmaker realizes
          profit if book balanced regardless of game's out-
          come, e.g., bettor bets $110, bookmaker bets $100 if
          a 10% vigorish.

     4.   Lay-off - done to tend towards balanced book, re-bet
          with another bookmaker.

5. Types of wagers:
   a. Straight wagers.
   b. Parlay wagers.
   c. Round Robins.
   d. Over-and-under - bets that total score will be over or under established line.
   e. Teasers - parlay bets with bettor given right to add fixed number of points to line on one or both of the teams and bet placed at reduced odds.
   f. Middles - bettor taking advantage of discrepancy in line of two bookmakers allowing him to bet on both sides of the game and to win both bets if the final point spread falls between these two lines.

B. Basketball - similar to football.

C. Hockey - usally a split line at even money or 11 to 10 or 6 to 5 odds. (For example: "Red Wings 1/2-1." Red Wings are -1, their opponent +1/2. The bookmaker hopes the final result will hit on the full number so that he will not have to make any payoffs on that team and can retain all money wagered on the other team. Wagering is also done in a manner like football (single line) or baseball (handicapping by money).)

D. Baseball:

   1. Line based on relative amounts of money put up by bettor rather than anticipated point spread.

   2. Examples:
      a. 6 - 7 means bettor on favorite risks $7.00 to win $5.00, bettor on underdog risks $5.00 to win $6.00 based on a $5.00 bet - 20 cents line.
      b. 40 - 50 or 140 - 150 means bettor on favorite risks 150 to win 100, bettor on underdog risks 100 to win 140 - 10-cent line.

      c. 8 - 9 means bettor on favorite risks $10.00 to win $8.00, bettor on underdog risks $9.00 to win $10.00 based on a $10.00 bet - 10-cent line.
      d. Football, baseball and basketball cards, pool cards, or lottery cards - no change in line daily, but very poor payoff odds.

VIII. Specialized materials:

A. Flash paper, erasable and water-soluble paper.

106

B. Backstraps, cheese boxes, blue boxes, black boxes.

C. Indented writing.

IX. Semi-destroyed materials: e.g. charred papers

X. Dice, Playing cards, Casino-type Games, Carnival-type Games and Private Games:

A. Detecting other than normal dice by comparing die to cube:

1. Roll characteristics of cube (edges and corners only touching surface until die comes to rest).

2. Alteration of edges, corners or surface or addition of weighting materials alters normal roll characteristics creating sides (and their spots) which show more frequently than normal dice. Use of spotting materials reactive to electrical field creating dice which will function in a desired way.

3. The necessity for altered dice (the inability of many to master manipulation of normal dice; the dice mechanic).

4. Shapes, flats, bevels (passers and miss-outs); edge work; loaded dice; tops and bottoms (miss-spots) (inability of players seeing more than three sides of die at any one time).

B. Playing cards:

1. Subtleties of marking cards (the need due to inability of many to master manipulation of unmarked cards for desired results).

2. Types of marks (additions and deletions of printed background, ultraviolet and prescription lenses which are reactive to special markings); punched, clipped, shaped cards; use of smooth and cambric cards in one deck.

C. Carnival types:

Many games essentially the same games with different names:

1. Common thread is throwing objects such as darts, hoops or rings, balls and coins in skill games, wheels, or needles, and using games of chance.

2. Varieties of games the manipulation of which is built in or up to the ingenuity of the operator.

107

RADIO ENGINEERING SECTION

        The Radio Engineering Section is responsible
for the supervision of the Bureau's radio and secure
teletype communications systems as well as for the development and/or procurement of many types of technical equipment
used in support of our investigative activities. In
addition, this section has the capability of examining
evidence of an electrical or electronic nature, conducting
anaylses of magnetic tape, and providing expert testimony
regarding findings.

        Some of the specific services which the Radio
Engineering Section can provide in the forensic area are:

  I. Examination of telephone devices

      A. Toll fraud

          1. "Blue box"

          2. "Black box"

          3. "Red box"

      B. To defeat records

          1. "Cheese box"

          2. Call diverters

      C. Intercepting communications

          1. Illegal equipment attached to telephone line
              to monitor and/or record third party conversation

          2. Illegal radio equipment capable of intercepting
              telephone communications and transmitting to remote
              location

 II. Examination of clandestine radio devices

III. Magnetic tape analysis

      A. Video

          1. Enhancement of image quality.

          2. Production of stills.

B. Audio

    1. Enhancement of audio intelligibility.

    2. Electronic comparison of recorded sounds in order to identify sound source.

    3. Audio comparison to establish origin or legitimacy.

C. Comparison of audiospectrograms (Voiceprint comparisons).

D. Audio and video comparisons of known and suspect tapes in copyright violation matters.

PART IV

COLLECTION AND PRESERVATION OF PHYSICAL EVIDENCE

I. Definition of evidence:

  A. Webster: That which is legally submitted to a competent tribunal as a means of ascertaining the truth of any alleged matter of fact under investigation before it.

  B. "Physical," "real," "tangible," "laboratory," "latent," are all adjectives to describe the type of evidence which the FBI Laboratory and Identification Divisions examine.

  C. Anything which a suspect leaves at a crime scene or takes from the scene or which may be otherwise connected with the crime.

II. Purpose of collection and examination of physical evidence:

  A. Aid in solution of case:

    1. Develop M.O.'s or show similar M.O.'s.

    2. Develop or identify suspects.

    3. Prove or disprove an alibi.

    4. Connect or eliminate suspects.

    5. Identify loot, contraband, illegal whiskey.

    6. Provide leads.

  B. Prove an element of the offense:

    1. Safe insulation, glass or building materials on suspect's clothing may prove entry.

2. Stomach contents, bullets, residue at scene of fire, semen, blood, toolmarks may all prove elements of certain offenses.

3. Safe insulation on tools **may** be sufficient to prove violation of possession of burglary tools statutes.

C. To prove theory of a case:

1. Soil, footprints may show how many were at scene.

2. Auto paint on clothing may show that person was hit by car instead of otherwise injured.

III. Crime Scene Search.

Defined as a planned, coordinated legal search by competent law enforcement officers to locate physical evidence or witnesses to the crime under investigation. To be effective:

A. Conduct preliminary examination of scene - PROTECT AREA!

B. Photograph scene (See section on Crime Scene Photography)

C. Sketch the scene.

D. Conduct search and collect the evidence.

IV. Collection of physical evidence (five things to keep in mind):

A. Obtain it legally:

1. Warrant.

2. Consent.

3. Incidental to arrest.

B. Describe it in notes:

1. Location, circumstances, how obtained.

2. Date, chain of custody.

3. How identified.

C. Identify it properly:

1. Use initials, date, case number.

110

2. Preferably on evidence itself. Liquids, soils, tiny fragments must be placed in suitable container, sealed and marked on outside.

D. Package it properly. One case to one box:

1. Use suitable containers such as round pillboxes, plastic vials, glass or plastic containers, strong cardboard cartons.

2. Seal securely against leakage.

3. Package each item separately - avoid even appearance of leakage or contamination.

4. If wet or bearing blood, air-dry before packaging (except arson cases where hydrocarbons are present).

E. Maintain chain of custody - keep it short:

1. Same person or persons should find, seal, initial and send evidence, if possible.

2. Maintain in locked vault, cabinet or room until shipped.

3. Send by railway express, air express, registered mail, registered air mail or personal delivery to Laboratory or Identification Division (there is no way to trace parcel post, certified mail or regular mail).

V. How to request an FBI Laboratory or Fingerprint examination: (See Page 115 for sample letter.)

A. All requests should be made by letter, in duplicate.

To: Director
Federal Bureau of Investigation
Washington, D. C. 20535

Marked: "ATTENTION: FBI Laboratory" or "ATTENTION: FBI Identification Division, Latent Fingerprint Section" in accordance with the following:

1. If evidence is for Laboratory or combined Laboratory-Fingerprint examination it should be marked "ATTENTION FBI Laboratory."

2. If evidence is <u>exclusively</u> for fingerprint examination mark "ATTENTION: FBI Identification Division, Latent Fingerprint Section."

B. Use additional copies of this letter of request as "Invoices" for separate shipment of evidence (see Part VI, B.).

C. Information in letter should include:

1. Complete names of all suspects and victims for indexing purposes.

2. Identify nature of violation or type of crime (character of case).

3. Date and place of crime.

4. Brief facts of case insofar as they pertain to the requested examinations - such as whether soil is from filled area, whether evidence was weathered or otherwise altered, whether preservative was added to blood or whether evidence is in the form in which it was at time of crime. Include photos if you feel they will assist.

5. How evidence is being sent (herewith or under separate cover - see Part VI).

6. List of evidence correlated with notes on wrappings of individual items, if appropriate.

7. What examinations or comparisons are to be conducted.

8. Whether to be compared with evidence in other <u>specific</u> cases.

9. Make reference to previous correspondence in this or related case, if any.

10. State what disposition should be made of the evidence.

11. If submitted for Laboratory examination, include statement certifying that same evidence has not

and will not be subjected to examination by other experts for the prosecution in the same scientific field. (See page 5, D, 1 for exceptions.) This statement not required regarding fingerprint evidence.

    12. Include statement as to whether any civil action has been specifically indicated by interested parties.

    13. Whether expeditious examination is needed. Caution: This treatment should not be _routinely_ requested.

VI. Dependent on size and type, evidence may be submitted:

A. Herewith.

    1. Certain small items of evidence, such as a fraudelent check or latent lifts, may be submitted along with the letter of request. This method limited to items not endangered by transmission in an envelope.

    2. Letter of request would state "Submitted herewith are the following items of evidence."

B. Under separate cover. Generally used for shipment of numerous and/or bulky items of evidence. Letter of request would state "Submitted under separate cover by (method of shipment) are the following items of evidence."

    1. Submit letter of request, in duplicate, by appropriate mailing method. (See Part V, this Section, on contents of letter.)

    2. Pack bulky evidence securely in box.

    3. Seal box and mark as evidence. Mark "Latent" if necessary.

    4. Place copy of transmittal letter (letter of request) in envelope and mark "Invoice."

5. Attach envelope containing "Invoice" to <u>outside</u> of sealed box.

6. Wrap sealed box in outside wrapper and <u>seal</u> with gummed paper. Attach any necessary labels.

7. Address to: Director
   Federal Bureau of Investigation
   Washington, D. C. 20535

   And marked to attention of appropriate FBI Division (See V, A, 1 and 2 of this section)

8. If packing box is wood -- tack invoice envelope to top under a clear plastic cover.

VII. Steps an officer should take before calling an FBI Laboratory or Latent Fingerprint expert to testify:

A. Ascertain whether the expert is a necessary witness. Is his testimony material? Can report be stipulated to by Defense?

B. Advise the Bureau when and where the trial is to be held as far in advance as possible in order to avoid conflicts with other commitments.

C. Advise regarding the expected duration of the trial and the exact date on which the expert will be needed.

D. Arrange for a conference between the prosecutor and the expert prior to the time the expert takes the stand and arrange for the expert's early release after testifying

E. Furnish the names of opposing experts, if any, and ascertain whether the prosecutor contemplates using any other experts. (See page 5, D, 3 for testimony policy.)

SAMPLE LETTER TO FBI LABORATORY

USE OFFICIAL LETTERHEAD

Police Headquarters
Right City, State (Zip Code)
March 17, 19--

Director
Federal Bureau of Investigation
U. S. Department of Justice
Washington, D. C. 20535

ATTENTION: FBI LABORATORY

Dear Sir:

RE: GUY PIDGIN, SUSPECT
EMPALL MERCHANDISE MART
BURGLARY

Sometime during the early morning of March 16, 19--, someone entered the Empall Merchandise Mart through an unlocked side window and made an unsuccessful attempt to rip open the safe. The outer layer of metal on the safe door had been pried loose from the upper right corner and bent outward ripping the metal along the top and down the side of the safe about 12" each way. The burglar may have been scared away because the job was not completed. Investigation led us to one Guy Pidgin who denies complicity. He voluntarily let us take his shoes and trousers and a crowbar that was under his bed in his rooming house.

I am sending by railway express a package containing the following evidence in this case:

1. One pair of shoes obtained from Guy Pidgin
2. A pair of grey flannel trousers obtained from Guy Pidgin
3. One 28" crowbar obtained from Guy Pidgin
4. Safe insulation taken from door of safe at Empall Merchandise Mart
5. Piece of bent metal approximately 12" x 12" taken from door of safe at Empall Merchandise Mart. In order to differentiate the two sides cut by us, we have placed adhesive tape on them.
6. Chips of paint taken from the side of safe
7. Fingerprint card for Guy Pidgin
8. Ten transparent lifts

It will be appreciated if you will examine the shoes and trousers to see if there is any safe insulation on them and to see if there are any paint chips on them that match the paint taken from the safe. Also, we would be interested to know whether it is possible to determine if the crowbar was used to open the safe. Examine items 5 and 8 to determine if latent fingerprints are present. If present, compare with item 7.

This evidence which should be returned to us, has not been examined by any other expert.

Very truly yours,

James T. Wixling
Chief of Police

REPORT
of the

FBI LABORATORY

FEDERAL BUREAU OF INVESTIGATION
WASHINGTON, D. C. 20535

To: Mr. James T. Wixling
Chief of Police
Right City, State (Zip Code)

March 22, 19--

FBI FILE NO. 95-67994

LAB. NO. PC-C4800 RF PD ST

Re:

GUY PIDGIN, SUSPECT;
EMPALL MERCHANDISE MART;
BURGLARY

YOUR NO.

Examination requested by: Addressee

Reference: Letter dated 3/17/--

Examination requested: Microscopic - Instrumental Analyses - Toolmarks

Specimens:

Q1   Right shoe belonging to GUY PIDGIN (your item 1)
Q2   Left shoe belonging to GUY PIDGIN (your item 1)
Q3   Pair of gray flannel trousers belonging to GUY PIDGIN
           (your item 2)
Q4   28" crowbar belonging to GUY PIDGIN (your item 3)
Q5   Piece of bent metal from door of safe (your item 5)

K1   Insulation from safe door at EMPALL MERCHANDISE MART
           (your item 4)
K2   Paint from front and side of safe at EMPALL MERCHANDISE
           MART (your item 6)

Also Submitted: 1 fingerprint card and ten transparent lifts
                      (your items 7 and 8)

This examination has been made with the understanding that the evidence is connected with an official
investigation of a criminal matter and that the Laboratory report will be used for official purposes only, related
to the investigation or a subsequent criminal prosecution. Authorization cannot be granted for the use of the
Laboratory report in connection with a civil proceeding.

Clarence M. Kelley
Director

Page 1

(Over)

Result of examination:

The insulation from the safe at the EMPALL MERCHANDISE MART, Kl, is a vermiculite type used by several leading safe manufacturers.

Particles of vermiculite safe insulation similar to Kl were found in and on the shoes, Ql and Q2, on the crowbar, Q4, and in the debris removed from the gray trousers, Q3. The particles of safe insulation on or in Ql, Q2, Q4 and Q3 either came from the safe represented by Kl or from another safe containing the same kind of insultion as Kl.

The paint chips, K2, from the safe consisted of five layers of paint:

(1) Dark green enamel
(2) Light green enamel
(3) Gray enamel
(4) Black lacquer
(5) Red primer

The Q3 trousers contained chips of paint consisting of five layers of paint similar in colors, layer structure, texture and composition to the K2 paint and could have come from the same source as K2 or another surface painted in a similar manner with similar paint.

The Q4 crowbar has smears of green paint on it similar to the top two layers of paint of K2 and the smears could have come from the same source as K2.

The Q5 piece of metal had no toolmarks of value for comparison with the Q4 crowbar.

The evidence in this case is being returned to you under separate cover by registered mail. The "Also Submitted" items will be the subject of a separate report

Page 2
PC-C4800 RF

FEDERAL BUREAU OF INVESTIGATION
Washington, D. C. 20537

REPORT
of the

IDENTIFICATION DIVISION
LATENT FINGERPRINT SECTION

YOUR FILE NO.
FBI FILE NO. 95-67994
LATENT CASE NO. A-73821

March 22, 19--

REGISTERED

TO: Mr. James T. Wixling
Chief of Police
Right City, State (Zip Code)

RE: GUY PIDGIN;
EMPALL MERCHANDISE MART
RIGHT CITY, STATE
MARCH 16, 19--
BURGLARY

REFERENCE: Letter March 17, 19--
EXAMINATION REQUESTED BY: Addressee
SPECIMENS: Piece of bent metal, Q5
Ten transparent lifts
Fingerprints of Guy Pidgin, FBI #213762J9

Four latent fingerprints of value were developed on the piece of metal, Q5. Seven latent fingerprints of value appear on three lifts marked "safe door" and five latent fingerprints of value appear on two lifts marked "side window." No additional latent prints of value appear on the remaining lifts.

Twelve of the latent fingerprints are not identical with the fingerprints of Guy Pidgin, FBI #213762J9. For the results of the additional comparisons conducted see the attached page.

Photographs of the unidentified latent fingerprints have been prepared for our files and will be available for any additional comparisons you may desire.

Clarence M. Kelley, Director

THIS REPORT IS FURNISHED FOR OFFICIAL USE ONLY

118

Mr. James T. Wixling   March 22, 19--

    Should you desire the assistance of one of the FBI's
fingerprint experts in the trial of this case, we should be
notified in ample time to permit the necessary arrangements.
This report should be used, however, if legal considerations
permit, in lieu of the appearance of our expert in any pre-
trial action such as a preliminary hearing or grand jury
hearing. Our representative cannot be made available to testify if any other fingerprint expert is to present testimony on
the same point, that is, that the impressions in question are
identical.

    The lifts and the fingerprints of Pidgin are enclosed
The fingerprints of Pidgin should be retained in your file for
any future possible court action in this case. The results of
the laboratory examinations, as well as the disposition of the
piece of metal, Q5, are the subjects of a separate report.

Enclosures (11)

Page 2
LCA-73821

Re: GUY PIDGIN, FBI #213762J9

Four latent fingerprints developed on a piece of metal, designated Q5, have been identified as finger impressions of Pidgin.

Proper Sealing of Evidence

The method shown below permits access to the invoice letter without breaking the inner seal.
This allows the person entitled to receive the evidence to receive it in a sealed condition just
as it was packed by the sender

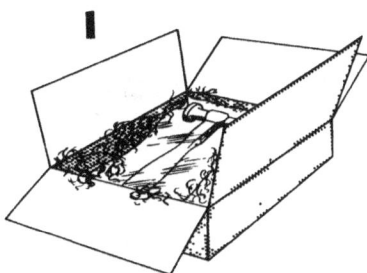

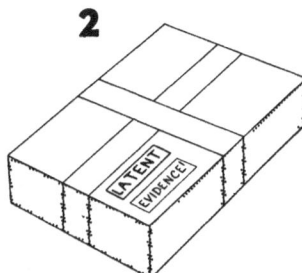

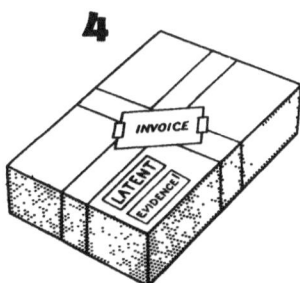

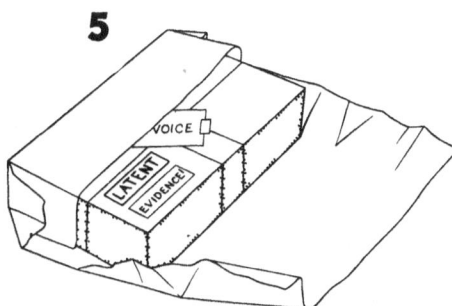

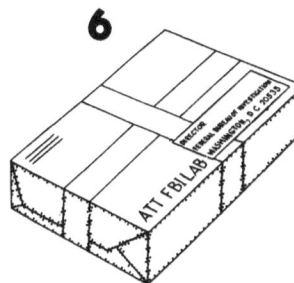

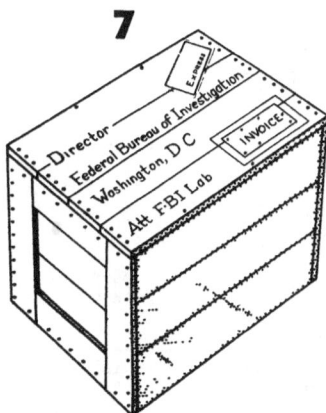

1. Pack bulk evidence securely in box.
2. __Seal__ box and mark as evidence.
   Mark "Latent" if necessary.
3. Place copy of transmittal letter in envelope
   and mark "Invoice."
4. Stick envelope to __outside__ of sealed box.
5. Wrap sealed box in outside wrapper and
   __seal__ with gummed paper.
6. Address to Director Federal Bureau of Investigation Washington, D. C 20535 and mark
   "Attention FBI Laboratory."
7. If packing box is wooden -- tack invoice
   envelope to top under a clear plastic cover.

121

CHART TO BE USED IN SUBMITTING

| SPECIMEN | IDENTIFICATION | AMOUNT DESIRED | |
		STANDARD	EVIDENCE
Abrasives, including carborundum, emery, sand, etc.	On outside of container. Type of material. Date obtained. Name or initials	Not less than one ounce	All
Acids	Same as above	One pint	All to one pint
Adhesive tape	Same as above	Recovered roll	All
Alkalies -- caustic soda, potash, ammonia, etc.	Same as above	One pint liquid One pound solid	All to one pint All to one pound
Ammunition (Cartridges)	Same as above		
Anonymous letters, extortion letters, bank robbery notes	Initial and date each document unless legal aspects or good judgment dictates otherwise.		All
Blasting caps	On outside of container. Type of material, date obtained, and name or initials.		All
Blood: 1. Liquid Known samples	Use adhesive tape on outside of test tube. Name of donor, date taken, doctor's name, name or initials of submitting Agent or officer	1/6 ounce (5cc) collected in sterile test tube	All
2. Drowning cases	Same as above	Two specimens: one from each side of heart	All
3. Small quantities: a. Liquid Questioned samples	Same as above as applicable		All to 1/6 ounce (5cc)
b. Dry stains Not on fabrics	On outside of pillbox or plastic vial. Type of specimen date secured, name or initials.		As much as possible

----
NOTE: This chart is not intended to be all-inclusive. If evidence to be submitted is not found herein, consult the specimen list for an item most similar in nature and submit accordingly.

PRESERVATION	WRAPPING AND PACKING	TRANSMITTAL	MISCELLANEOUS
None	Use containers, such as ice-cream box, pillbox, or plastic vial. Seal to prevent any loss.	Registered mail or RR or air express	Avoid use of envelopes
None	Plastic or all-glass bottle. Tape in stopper. Pack in sawdust, glass, or rock wool. Use bakelite- or paraffin-lined bottle for hydrofluoric acid.	RR express only	Label acids, glass, corrosive.
None	Place on waxed paper or cellophane.	Registered mail	Do not cut, wad, or distort.
None	Plastic or glass bottle with rubber stopper held with adhesive tape	RR express only	Label alkali, glass, corrosive.
None	"Shipping of Live Ammunition," p.45 and p.132. Note: Outside shipping container must be made of wood or fiberboard, per Department of Transportation regulations.	RR or air express	Unless specific exam of cartridge is essential, do not submit. Shipping is costly.
Do not handle with bare hands.	Place in proper enclosure envelope and seal with "Evidence" tape or transparent cellophane tape. Flap side of envelope should show (1) wording "Enclosure (s) to Bureau from (name of submitting office)," (2) title of case, (3) brief description of contents, and (4) file number, if known. Staple to original letter of transmittal	Registered mail	Advise if evidence should be treated for latent fingerprints.

Should not be forwarded until advised to do so by the Laboratory. Packing instructions will be given at that time.

PRESERVATION	WRAPPING AND PACKING	TRANSMITTAL	MISCELLANEOUS
Sterile tube only. NO REFRIGERANT.	Wrap in cotton, soft paper. Place in mailing tube or suitably strong mailing carton.	Airmail, special delivery, registered	Submit immediately. Don't hold awaiting additional items for comparison.
Same as above	Same as above	Airmail, special delivery, registered	Same as above
Allow to dry thoroughly on nonporous surface	Same as above	Airmail, special delivery, registered	Collect by using eyedropper or clean spoon, transfer to nonporous surface. Allow to dry and submit in pillbox.
Keep dry.	Seal to prevent leakage.	Registered mail	

CHART TO BE USED IN SUBMITTING

| SPECIMEN | IDENTIFICATION | AMOUNT DESIRED | |
		STANDARD	EVIDENCE
4. Stained clothing, fabric, etc.	Use tag or mark directly on clothes. Type of specimens, date secured, name or initials.		As found
Bullets (not cartridges)	Initials on base, nose or mutilated area		All found
Cartridges (live ammunition)	Initials on outside of case near bullet end	See Note p.45, re "Shipping of Live Ammunition"	All found
Cartridge cases (shells)	Initials preferably on inside near open end or on outside near open end.		All
Charred or burned	On outside of container indicate fragile nature of evidence, date obtained, name or initials.		All
Checks (fraudulent)	See anonymous letters		All
Check protector, rubber stamp and dater stamp sets, known standards Note: Send actual device when possible.	Place name or initials, date, name of make and model, etc., on sample impressions.	Obtain several copies in full word-for-word order of each questioned check-writer impression. If unable to forward rubber stamps, prepare numerous samples with different degrees of pressure.	
Clothing	Mark directly on garment or use string tag. Type of evidence, name or initials, date.		All
Codes, ciphers, and foreign language material	As anonymous letters		All

PRESERVATION	WRAPPING AND PACKING	TRANSMITTAL	MISCELLANEOUS
If wet when found, dry by hanging. USE NO HEAT TO DRY. No preservative.	Each article wrapped separately and identified on outside of package. Place in strong box packed to prevent shifting of contents.	Registered mail or air or RR express	
None. Unnecessary handling obliterates marks	Pack tightly in cotton or soft paper in pill, match or powder box. Label outside of box as to contents.	Registered mail	
None	Same as above	RR express or air express	Live ammunition cannot be sent through U.S. mails. See "Shipping of Live Ammunition," p.45.
None	Same as above	Registered mail	
None	Pack in rigid container between layers of cotton	Registered mail	Added moisture, with atomizer or otherwise, not recommended.
None	See anonymous letters	Registered mail	Advise what parts questioned or known. Furnish physical description of subject.
None	See anonymous letters or bulky evidence wrapping instructions	Registered mail	Do not disturb inking mechanisms on printing devices.
None	Each article individually wrapped with identification written on outside of package. Place in strong container.	Registered or RR or air express	Leave clothing whole. Do not cut out stains. If wet, hang in room to dry before packing.
None	As anonymous letters	As anonymous letters	Furnish all background and technical information pertinent to examination.

CHART TO BE USED IN SUBMITTING

SPECIMEN	IDENTIFICATION	AMOUNT DESIRED STANDARD	EVIDENCE
Drugs:			
1. Liquids	Affix label to bottle in which found including name or initials and date.		All to one pint
2. Powders, pills, and solids	On outside of pillbox. Name or initials and date.		All to 1/4 pound
Dynamite and other explosives	Consult the FBI Laboratory and follow their telephonic or telegraphic instructions.		
Fibers	On outside of sealed container or on object to which fibers are adhering	Entire garment or other cloth item	All
Firearms	Mark inconspicuously as if it were your own. String tag gun, noting complete description on tag. Investigative notes should reflect how and where gun marked.		All
Flash paper	Initials and date	One sheet	All
Fuse, safety	Attach string tag or gummed paper label, name or initials, and date.	One foot	All
Gasoline	On outside of all-metal container, label with type of material, name or initials, and date.	One quart	All to one gallon
Glass fragments	Adhesive tape on each piece. Name or initials and date on tape. Separate questioned and known.		All
Glass particles	Name or initials, date on outside of sealed container	3" piece of broken item	All
Gunshot Residue Tests:			
1. Paraffin	On outside of container. Type of material, date, and name or initials.		All
2. On cloth	Attach string tag or mark directly. Type of material, date, and name or initials.		All
Hair	On outside of container. Type of material, date, and name or initials.	Dozen or more full length hairs from different parts of head and/or body.	All

PRESERVATION	WRAPPING AND PACKING	TRANSMITTAL	MISCELLANEOUS
None	If bottle has no stopper, transfer to glass-stoppered bottle and seal with adhesive tape.	Registered mail or RR or air express	Mark "Fragile." Determine alleged normal use of drug and if prescription, check with druggist to determine supposed ingredients.
None	Seal to prevent any loss by use of tape.	Registered mail or RR or air express	
None	Folded paper or pillbox. Seal edges and openings with tape.	Registered mail	Do not place loose in envelope.
Keep from rusting.	Wrap in paper and identify contents of package. Place in cardboard box or wooden box.	Registered mail or RR or air express	Unload all weapons before shipping.
Fireproof, vented location away from any other combustible materials. If feasible, immerse in water.	Individual polyethylene envelopes double wrapped in manila envelopes. Inner wrapper sealed with paper tape.	Five sheets (8 x 10½) surface mail parcel post. Over 5 sheets telephonically consult FBI Laboratory.	Mark inner wrapper "Flash Paper Flammable."
None	Place in manila envelope, box, or suitable container.	Registered mail or RR or air express	
Fireproof container	Metal container packed in wooden box	RR express only	
Avoid chipping.	Wrap each piece separately in cotton. Pack in strong box to prevent shifting and breakage. Identify contents.	Registered mail or RR or air express	Mark "Fragile."
None	Place in pillbox, plastic or glass vial; seal and protect against breakage	Registered mail	Do not use envelopes.
Containers must be free of any nitrate-containing substance. Keep cool.	Wrap in waxed paper or place in sandwich bags. Lay on cotton in a substantial box. Place in a larger box packed with absorbent material.	Registered mail	Use "Fragile" label. Keep cool.
None	Place fabric flat between layers of paper and then wrap, so that no residue will be transferred or lost.	Registered mail	Avoid shaking
None	Folded paper or pillbox. Seal edges and openings with tape.	Registered mail	Do not place loose in envelope.

CHART TO BE USED IN SUBMITTING

SPECIMEN	IDENTIFICATION	AMOUNT DESIRED	
		STANDARD	EVIDENCE
Handwriting and hand printing, known standards	Name or initials, date, from whom obtained, and voluntary statement should be included in appropriate place.	See footnote.*	
Matches	On outside of container. Type of material, date, and name or initials.	One to two books of paper. One full box of wood.	All
Medicines (See drugs.)			
Metal	Same as above	One pound	All to one pound
Oil	Same as above	One quart together with specifi- cations	All to one quart
Obliterated, eradicated, or indented writing	See anonymous letters.		All
Organs of body	On outside of container. Victim's name, date of death, date of autopsy, name of doctor, name or initials.		All to one pound
Paint: 1. Liquid	On outside of container. Type of material, origin if known, date, name or initials.	Original unopened container up to 1 gallon if possible	All to ¼ pint
2. Solid (paint chips or scrapings)	Same as above	At least ½ sq. inch of solid, with all layers represented	All. If on small object send object.

*Duplicate the original writing conditions as to text, speed, slant, size of paper, size of writing, type of writing instruments, etc. Do not allow suspect to see questioned writing. Give no instructions as to spelling, punctuation, etc. Remove each sample from sight as soon as completed. Suspect should fill out blank check forms in cases (FD-352). In hand printing cases, both upper- (capital) and lower-case (small) samples should be obtained In forgery cases, obtain sample signatures of the person whose name is forged. Have writer prepare some specimens with hand not normally used. Obtain undictated handwriting when feasible.

PRESERVATION	WRAPPING AND PACKING	TRANSMITTAL	MISCELLANEOUS
None	See anonymous letters.	Registered mail	
Keep away from fire.	Metal container and packed in larger package to prevent shifting. Matches in box or metal container packed to prevent friction between matches.	RR express or registered mail	"Keep away from fire" label
Keep from rusting.	Use paper boxes or containers. Seal and use strong paper or wooden box.	Registered mail or RR or air express	Melt number, heat treatment, and other specifications of foundry if available
Keep away from fire.	Metal container with tight screw top. Pack in strong box using excelsior or similar material.	RR express only	DO NOT USE DIRT OR SAND FOR PACKING MATERIAL.
None	See anonymous letters.	Registered mail	Advise whether bleaching or staining methods may be used. Avoid folding.
None to evidence. Dry ice in package not touching glass jars.	Plastic or all-glass containers (glass jar with glass top)	RR or air express	"Fragile" label. Keep cool. Metal top containers must not be used. Send autopsy report.
None	Friction-top paint can or large-mouth, screw-top jars. If glass, pack to prevent breakage. Use heavy corrugated paper or wooden box.	Registered mail or RR or air express	
Wrap so as to protect smear.	If small amount, round pillbox or small glass vial with screw top. Seal to prevent leakage. Envelopes not satisfactory.	Registered mail or RR or air express	Do not pack in cotton. Avoid contact with adhesive materials.

SPECIMEN	IDENTIFICATION	AMOUNT DESIRED	
		STANDARD	EVIDENCE
Plaster casts of tire treads and shoe prints	On back before plaster hardens. Location, date, and name or initials.	Send in shoes and tires of suspects. Photographs and sample impressions are usually not suitable for comparison.	All shoe prints; entire circumference of tire
Powder patterns (See gunpowder tests.)			
Rope, twine, and cordage	On tag or container. Type of material, date, name or initials.	One yard	All
Safe insulation or soil	On outside of container. Type of material, date, name or initials.	$\frac{1}{2}$ pound	All to one pound
Shoe print lifts (impressions on hard surfaces)	On lifting tape or paper attached to tape. Name or initials and date.	Photograph before making lift of dust impression.	All
Tools	On tools or use string tag. Type of tool, identifying number, date, name or initials.		All
Toolmarks	On object or on tag attached to or on opposite end from where toolmarks appear. Name or initials and date.	Send in the tool. If impractical, make several impressions on similar material as evidence using entire marking area of tool.	All
Typewriting, known standards	Place name or initials, date, serial number, name of make and model, etc., on specimens.	Obtain at least one copy in full word-for-word order of questioned typewriting. Also include partial copies in light, medium, and heavy degrees of touch. Also carbon paper samples of every character on the keyboard.	
Urine or water	On outside of container. Type of material, name of subject, date taken, name or initials.	Preferably all urine voided over a period of 24 hours	All
Wire (See also toolmarks.)	On label or tag. Type of material, date, name or initials.	Three feet (Do not kink.)	All (Do not kink.)
Wood	Same as above	One foot	All

130

PRESERVATION	WRAPPING AND PACKING	TRANSMITTAL	MISCELLANEOUS
Allow casts to cure (dry) before wrapping.	Wrap in paper and cover with suitable packing material to prevent breakage. Do not wrap in unventilated plastic bags.	Registered mail or RR or air express	Use "Fragile" label. Mix approximately four pounds of plaster to quart of water.
	Wrap securely.	Registered mail	
	Use containers, such as pillbox, or plastic vial. Seal to prevent any loss.	Registered mail or RR or air express	Avoid use of glass containers and envelopes.
None	Prints in dust are easily damaged. Fasten print or lift to bottom of a box so that nothing will rub against it.	Registered mail	Always rope off crim scene area until shoe prints or tire treads are located and preserved.
	Wrap each tool in paper. Use strong cardboard or wooden box with tools packed to prevent shifting.	Registered mail or RR or air express	
Cover ends bearing toolmarks with soft paper and wrap with strong paper to protect ends.	After marks have been protected, wrap in strong wrapping paper, place in strong box, and pack to prevent shifting.	Registered mail or RR or air express	
None	See anonymous letters.	Registered mail	Examine ribbon for evidence of questioned message thereon. For carbon paper samples either remove ribbon or place in stencil position.
None. Use any clean bottle with leakproof stopper.	Bottle surrounded with absorbent material to prevent breakage. Strong cardboard or wooden box.	Registered mail	
	Wrap securely.	Registered mail	Do not kink wire.
	Wrap securely.	Registered mail	

REGULATIONS FOR SHIPMENT OF SMALL-ARMS
AMMUNITION (CLASS C EXPLOSIVES) EXCERPTED FROM
"HAZARDOUS MATERIALS REGULATIONS OF THE
DEPARTMENT OF TRANSPORTATION"
(Tariff #29) - Effective 1/14/75

§173.100 Definitions of class C explosives. (a) Explosives,
class C, are defined as certain types of manufactured articles
which contain class A, or class B explosives, or both, as
components but in restricted quantities, and certain types of
fireworks. These explosives are further specifically described
in this section.

(b) Small arms ammunition is fixed ammunition consisting
of a metallic, plastic composition, or paper cartridge case, a
primer and a propelling charge, with or without bullet, projectile
shot, tear gas material, tracer components, or incendiary
compositions, or mixtures and is further limited to the following:

(1) Ammunition designed to be fired from a pistol,
revolver, rifle, or shotgun held by the hand or to the shoulder.

(2) Ammunition of caliber less than 20 millimeters with
incendiary, solid, inert or empty projectiles (with or without
tracers), designed to be fired from machine guns or cannons.

(3) Blank cartridges including canopy remover cartridges,
starter cartridges, and seat ejector cartridges, containing not
more than 500 grains of propellant powder, provided that such
cartridges shall be incapable of functioning en masse as a result
of the functioning of any single cartridge in the container or as
a result of exposure to external flame.

(4) Twenty millimeter ammunition other than specified in
§173.53 (q).

§173.101 Small-Arms ammunition. (a) Small-arms ammunition
must be packed in pasteboard or other inside boxes, or in
partitions designed to fit snugly in the outside container, or
must be packed in metal clips. The partitions and metal clips
must be so designed as to protect the primers from accidental
injury. The inside boxes, partitions and metal clips must be
packed in securely closed strong outside wooden or fiberboard
boxes or metal containers. Blank Industrial Power Load cartridges
similar to the 22 long rim-fire cartridge, may be packed in
bulk in securely closed fiberboard boxes.

(b)   Small-arms ammunition in pasteboard or other inside
boxes, in addition to containers prescribed in paragraph (a)
of this section, may be shipped when packed in the same outside
container with nonexplosive and nonflammable articles; or
with small-arms primers or percussion caps in quantity not
to exceed 5 pounds. The weight of the small-arms ammunition
packed with other articles must not exceed 55 pounds in
outside fiberboard box, or 75 pounds in outside wooden box.
The outside package must be a securely closed strong wooden or
fiberboard container.

(c)   Each outside package must be plainly marked "SMALL-
ARMS AMMUNITION".

(d)   Outside containers of cartridges with tear gas
material must in addition to marking prescribed herein be marked
"TEAR GAS CARTRIDGES" and must be labeled with "TEAR GAS" label.
(See §173.409 (a) (3) of this part for label.)

(e)   No restrictions, other than proper description,
packing and marking for small-arms ammunition and additional
marking and labeling for tear gas cartridges are prescribed in
this part for the transportation of small-arms ammunition and tear
gas cartridges.

(f)   Shipments of small-arms ammunition, including broken
lots which have lost their identity (lot number identification),
may be shipped loosely packed in securely closed strong wooden
boxes or metal boxes, in carload or truckload lots, when
shipments are made by or for the Departments of the Army,
Navy or Air Force of the United States Government to depots or
manufacturing plants for reprocessing or demilitarization.
Seriously deteriorated ammunition or ammunition damaged to the
point of exposing incendiary or tracer composition, spillage
of propellant powder, or ammunition with other hazardous defects
must not be shipped. Each outside package must be plainly
marked "SMALL-ARMS AMMUNITION."

§173.101a Cartridges, practice ammunition.   (a) Cartridges,
practice ammunition must be packaged in pasteboard or other
inside boxes, or in partitions designed to fit snugly in the
outside packaging or must be packed in metal clips. The
partitions and metal clips must be so designed as to protect
the primers from accidental injury. The inside boxes, partitions,
and metal clips must be packaged in securely closed strong
outside wooden or fiberboard boxes or metal packagings.

(1)   Each package must be plainly marked "Cartridges,
Practice Ammunition."